REVOLUTIONARY WAR DAYS

American Kids in History™

REVOLUTIONARY WAR DAYS

Discover the Past with Exciting Projects, Games, Activities, and Recipes

David C. King

Illustrations by Cheryl Kirk Noll

John Wiley & Sons, Inc.

New York • Chichester • Weinheim • Brisbane • Singapore • Toronto

This book is printed on acid-free paper. ∞

Published by John Wiley & Sons, Inc.
Published simultaneously in Canada

Design: Michaelis/Carpelis Design Assoc., Inc.

The publisher and the author have made every reasonable effort to insure that the experiments and activities in this book are safe when conducted as instructed but assume no responsibility for any damage caused or sustained while performing the experiments or activities in this book. Parents, guardians, and/or teachers should supervise young readers who undertake the experiments and activities in this book.

Library of Congress Cataloging-in-Publication Data:
King, David C.
      Revolutionary War days: discover the past with exciting projects, games,
    activities, and recipes / David C. King.
         p. cm.—(American kids in history)
    ISBN 0-471-39308-8 (pbk. : alk. paper)
    1. United States—History—Revolution, 1775–1783—Social aspects—Study and teaching—Activity programs—Juvenile literature. 2. United States—History—Revolution, 1775–1783—Children—Study and teaching—Activity programs—Juvenile literature. 3. Children—United States—Social life and customs—18th century—Study and teaching—Activity programs—Juvenile literature. I. Title. II. Series.
E209 .K56 2001
973.3'1—dc21
                                                 00-059432
                                                 CIP

Printed in the United States of America

10 9 8 7 6 5 4 3 2 1

For Sharon

ACKNOWLEDGMENTS

Special thanks to the many people who made this book possible, including: Kate C. Bradford, Michelle Whelan, Sibylle Kazeroid, and the editorial staff of the Professional and Trade Division, John Wiley & Sons, Inc.; Susan E. Meyer and the staff of Roundtable Press, Inc.; Marianne Palladino and Irene Carpelis of Michaelis/Carpelis Design; Miriam Sarzin, for her copyediting; Sharon Flitterman-King and Diane Ritch for craft expertise; Cheryl Kirk Noll for the drawings; Steven Tiger, librarian, and the students of the Roe-Jan Elementary School, Hillsdale, New York; and, for research assistance, the staff members of the Great Barrington Public Library, the Atheneum (Pittsfield, Massachusetts), Old Sturbridge Village, and the Farmers Museum, Cooperstown, New York. Historical art courtesy of Dover Publications, Inc.

CONTENTS

REVOLUTIONARY WAR DAYS

INTRODUCTION

The American Revolution, 1775–1783

The Revolutionary War began in April 1775, when American colonists took up arms against the soldiers of their own ruler, King George III of England. The "Patriots," as they called themselves, were fighting to protest the unfairness of English rule, including taxes that were imposed on them, even though they had no representation in the British Government. A year later, the Patriots took an even more daring step: on July 4, 1776, the Continental Congress, representing all thirteen colonies, issued the Declaration of Independence. In this bold document, the colonists declared their independence from England. The former colonies declared themselves the thirteen free and independent United States of America.

Declaring independence was one thing; winning independence was another matter. England (which was also known as Great Britain following its union with Scotland and Wales) was by far the most powerful nation in the world. Against the large, well-trained British army, the Patriots had only the hastily assembled Continental Army, commanded by General George Washington, plus the state and local militia, made up of untrained citizen soldiers who could rarely stand up to a professional army.

The Patriots, however, were fighting for their homes, their freedom, and their right to govern themselves. And in 1778 they gained a powerful ally when France joined the war against Great Britain. The aid of the French was vital in gaining the final victory in the Battle of Yorktown (Virginia) in 1781, a victory that finally forced England to recognize America's independence.

For Americans during the Revolution, the war sometimes was very close. Many families had at least one person serving in the militia, the Continental Army, or the new Continental Navy. Battles were fought in every state, and the British also raided many towns for food, horses, and supplies. In addition, nearly one-third of the American people opposed independence and 100,000 of these "Loyalists" formed their own regiments and fought alongside the British. But throughout these struggles, American families maintained as normal a life as possible. They worked their farms, managed their shops, raised their children, and formed state governments. When peace finally came, they had succeeded in creating a new nation—the United States of America, a nation that has served as a model to the world ever since.

The Logans and the Wentworths

This book follows the Logan family of Virginia through the spring and summer of 1776, and the Wentworth family of Philadelphia through the autumn and winter of that same year. Although

the Logans and the Wentworths are not real families, their stories will show what life was like during the dramatic and exciting days of the Revolutionary War.

Eleven-year-old Joshua Logan lived with his family on a farm in the foothills of Virginia's Blue Ridge Mountains. In addition to growing a variety of farm crops, his parents, Frances and Jeremiah Logan, raised and trained saddle horses. Jeremiah was an officer in the Charlottesville militia regiment and, like most of their neighbors, he was a strong supporter of the Patriot cause. Militia duty and trading horses often kept Jeremiah away from home, so much of the farmwork fell to Joshua, his mother, and his sister Laurie, who was eight. The two youngest children—Diana, six, and Andrew, five—helped with tasks like feeding the horses and other farm animals. All of the children also had to keep up with their lessons, with the oldest helping the youngest. There was no school for many miles from their farm, but their mother was a strict teacher.

In the second part of the book, the story moves to Philadelphia, where the Wentworth family operated a lodging house. Peggy Wentworth, who had just turned twelve, loved the bustle and excitement of their four-story brick inn, with lodgers arriving and departing almost daily. Alexander Wentworth, Peggy's father, had lost a leg twenty years earlier fighting for the British in a war against France. He spent much of his time in the parlor serving coffee, cider, or wine to the lodgers and exchanging stories about war and politics. Peggy's mother, Martha Wentworth, managed the work of the house with the help of a cook and two servant girls who cleaned and served meals. Peggy also helped with the work except for twelve weeks in the winter when she attended Miss Carter's Academy for Young Ladies, where she studied sewing, music, and painting, as well as reading, penmanship, and Latin.

Peggy's parents thought the Revolution was wrong. They hoped that the Patriots would give up the war or that a British peace commission would arrange a peace without granting independence. Their oldest son, Robert, nineteen, went even further and planned to join a Loyalist regiment. Peggy, however, and her other brother, seventeen-year-old Thomas, quietly supported the Patriot cause, and Thomas even talked of joining Washington's Continental Army.

The Projects and Activities

As you follow the Logans and the Wentworths through the year 1776, you can try many of the activities kids like Joshua Logan and Peggy Wentworth might have done. Like them, you can make a punched-tin lantern, fashion a pair of moccasins, or use pegs to put together a small planter. You can try recipes for Independence Day shortcake or Christmas treats called chewy noels, and for fun you can make and play Ben Franklin's glass harmonica or pretend you're a Patriot trapped by the British in a game called Patriots and Redcoats. You'll be able to complete the projects with materials you have around your home or school, or that can be easily purchased at little cost. As you work on the activities, projects, and recipes, you'll feel the past come to life and you'll discover what it was like to be an American kid living in Revolutionary War days.

CHAPTER ONE

SPRING

Spring came early to the foothills overlooking Virginia's Shenandoah Valley in 1776, giving the Logan family and their neighbors a welcome early start on plowing and planting. Jeremiah Logan could also begin training some of the colts they had purchased over the winter.

When the first rush of spring work was finished, Jeremiah planned to deliver eight saddle horses to the Continental Army's headquarters outside Boston. He could also find out what was happening in the war. The Patriots had the main British army trapped in Boston and the British would soon have to abandon the city. But where would they strike next? And what about the great question of independence? Would the Continental Congress dare to make such a declaration? And if they did, could the Patriots win? All of the Logans' neighbors were eager to hear the news Jeremiah would bring back.

JOSHUA IN CHARGE

By the time his father left on the long journey to Boston, Joshua was no longer sad about being left behind. His father had explained to him that Joshua was now the man of the family and the only person Jeremiah could put in charge of the horses. Joshua took this new responsibility seriously. There was a lot to do and to remember. He had to be sure to exercise each horse regularly, for example, but not to feed them just before or just after he worked them. There was something special to remember about almost every horse, such as mixing chopped straw in the feed of any horse that was eating too much, like the little strawberry roan (a white colt with reddish markings). And some of his work involved instructing Laurie, Diana, and Andrew in such things as remembering to talk softly around the animals, but never to approach a horse silently because horses "spooked" easily.

Joshua's mother added to his feeling of being grown-up. First, she worked with him to shape a piece of felt into a three-cornered hat like the ones the men in the militia wore. Then she helped him sew two pieces of leather into a hunter's bag to go with the new rifle he had received on his birthday.

PROJECT HUNTER'S BAG

In the 1700s, a boy usually began learning to hunt by age ten or eleven and received his first musket or rifle at his next birthday. Since nine out of every ten Americans lived on farms or in small villages close to open countryside, hunting was a natural way to add to a family's food supply. To carry ammunition, the young man also received a powder horn and a sturdy hunter's bag. In frontier areas, hunting bags were usually made of buckskin (pale yellow deerskin), often with a fringe to match the fringe on a frontiersman's hunting shirt.

You can make your version of a hunter's bag out of felt, denim, or chamois (pronounced sham-my or cham-my). Chamois is much like buckskin and is available in the automotive section of most discount department stores. (Modern chamois cloth is often a factory-made fabric.) Use your hunter's bag to carry or collect things on hikes, or for storing and carrying small personal items.

MATERIALS

2 side panels of a large paper grocery bag, or a sheet
   of newsprint
ruler
pencil
scissors
2 pieces of chamois, light brown felt, or denim, each
   at least 15 inches by 9 inches

15 to 20 straight pins
large sewing needle
strong thread in color to match the fabric
button (brass or wood if possible)
hole punch

1. Place the sheets of grocery bag paper or newsprint on your work surface. With ruler and pencil, copy pattern A onto the paper. Cut out the pattern with scissors. Use pattern A and a ruler to make smaller pattern B, which will be 9 inches high instead of 15 inches. Cut out pattern B.

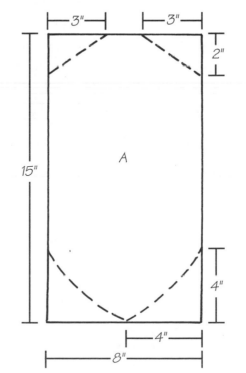

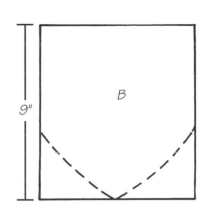

2. Spread the two pieces of chamois or other fabric on your work surface. Place pattern A on one piece of fabric, pattern B on the other. Position the patterns close to the edge of the fabric; this will leave enough extra fabric for you to cut two long, narrow pieces for straps.

3. Pin the patterns to the fabric and carefully trace around each pattern with pencil. Remove the patterns and cut out the two pieces.

4. Place the large piece of fabric on your work surface with the front (or right) side facing up. Position the smaller piece on top, with the front side facing down. Pin the two pieces together.

5. Thread a needle with about 20 inches of thread, pulling all but about 6 inches through the eye. Tie a double knot near the end of the longer part. Sew the bottom and two sides of the bag together, using a running stitch about ¼ inch from the edge. To sew a running stitch, bring the needle up at a, go down at b, come up again at c, down at d, and so on, as shown. When you've finished sewing the bottom and both sides, tie off the thread, cut off any extra, and remove the pins.

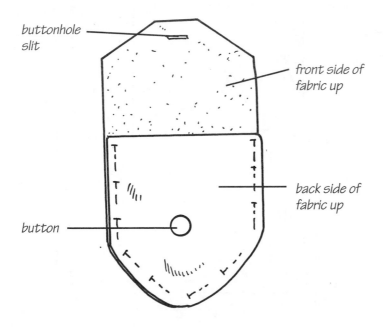

buttonhole slit

front side of fabric up

back side of fabric up

button

d   c   b   a

6. Turn the bag right side out. Use scissors to cut a 1-inch slit for a buttonhole in the top flap of the bag, as shown. (Use the point of the scissors to poke a hole to get the slit started.)

7. Fold the top flap down to close the bag. With a pencil, make a mark through the buttonhole onto the fabric underneath.

8. Open the bag and sew the button over the marked spot. Check to make sure the bag can be buttoned shut and make any necessary adjustments.

9. For straps, mark and cut out two strips at least 15 inches long and ¾ inch wide from the leftover chamois. Sew one strip to the back of the bag on either side, as shown.

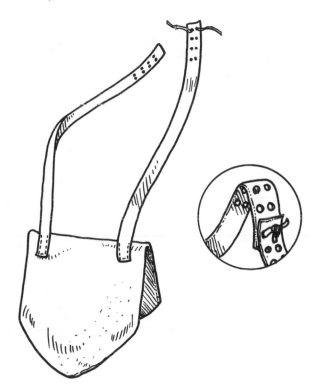

10. With a hole punch, make four or five pairs of holes in the ends of the straps, as shown in the drawing. Cut a small piece of fabric to make a

lace for tying the two straps together. With this device, you've reproduced the 1700s version of an adjustable strap!

11. If you want to add a strip of fringe to the flap of the bag, cut a piece of fabric about 9 inches long and 3 inches wide. With scissors, cut fringes into the fabric about 2 inches long, leaving about 1 inch of fabric for attaching the fringe to the bag. Sew the fringe piece to the bottom of the flap as shown. You've now re-created one of the standard pieces of equipment used by Patriot militiamen and frontier hunters.

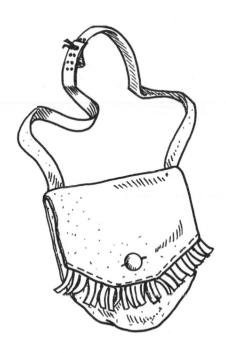

Muskets and Rifles

The standard weapon used by both British and Americans in the Revolutionary War was the musket. This was a heavy, clumsy gun that was not very accurate. Armies used them to fire heavy volleys, until close enough to use the deadly bayonets.

Many Patriots in frontier areas preferred a newer weapon—the rifle. This smaller, lighter weapon had spiral grooves, called rifles, cut into the barrel. The grooves made the bullet spin as it left the gun barrel, producing much greater accuracy than any musket, even at a distance. Loading the rifle, however, required slow, precise steps, making riflemen almost helpless when they were being attacked, especially since a bayonet could not be attached to a rifle. But when Patriot sharpshooters could fire from a distance, they took a heavy toll on the British and led some British soldiers to

think that every American was an expert marksman.

PROJECT THREE-CORNERED HAT

From about 1740 to 1800, the most common hat for men and boys was the tricorn—a three-cornered hat made of felt or beaver fur. Because most Patriot militiamen and soldiers in the Continental Army wore these three-sided hats, later generations had the impression that only Patriots had worn them, forgetting that the style was not unknown to the British and Loyalists.

In this activity, you'll make a simpler version of the tricorn by using a parlor game technique that became popular in Europe and America in the mid-1700s. The game, called chapeaugraphie (a French word meaning "writing with hats"), involved making a ring out of stiff fabric, then seeing how many different hat shapes could be made from it. By using this technique, you'll make a hat that looks very much like a Patriot's tricorn, although it will not have a crown. (If you wish, you can easily add a crown by attaching a baseball cap with the visor cut off.)

(*Note:* Adhesive for bonding fabric, such as Stitch Witchery, is available in the fabric or notions section of most discount department stores.)

MATERIALS

2 pieces of black or dark blue felt, each about 18 inches square
ruler
drawing compass (or 2 round plates: one 17 inches in diameter, the other 5½ inches)
pencil
white chalk, crayon, or colored pencil
scissors
iron-on adhesive for bonding fabric, or fabric glue (the two pieces can also be sewn together, by hand or sewing machine)
electric iron (for iron-on adhesive)

needle and thread in color to match fabric
black or dark blue baseball cap with visor removed (optional)

1. Spread one piece of felt on your work surface. Use a drawing compass (or a plate and pencil) to draw a circle about 17 inches in diameter. (If you use a plate, check the diameter with a ruler.) To make the line stand out clearly, go over it with white chalk, crayon, or colored pencil.

2. Cut out the circle with scissors. In the middle of the fabric, draw a smaller circle, about 5½ inches in diameter. Go over the line with your white marker, then cut out this inside circle.

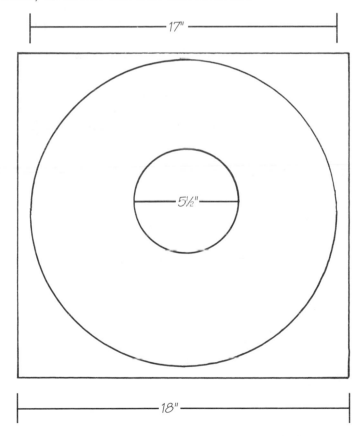

Tricorns with Ribbons

One of the many problems General Washington faced in creating the Continental Army was the matter of uniforms. Washington himself helped design the uniform in colors of dark blue, white, and buff (a light sand color). The problem was that thousands of these uniforms would have to be made and each uniform had to be made by hand. Even the weaving and dyeing of the cloth required hand labor.

Many months passed before the Continentals began to have the appearance of a real army with proper uniforms. Until then, when Washington's men went into battle, some wore their old militia uniforms, many were in civilian clothes, and the rifle regiments wore their fringed buckskin. The soldiers had no way of knowing which men were officers or what rank they held, so Washington devised a system of colored ribbons—a different color for each rank, from general down to sergeant. In order for the ribbons to be visible from a distance, most officers sewed them to their tricorns.

3. Put this ring on your head like a flat hat to see how well it fits. If necessary, use scissors to make the hole a little larger until the fit is comfortable.

4. Place the ring on top of the second piece of felt and use it as a pattern to make a second ring exactly the size of the first. Cut out this second ring.

5. Bond the two rings, one on top of the other, using the bonding adhesive, fabric glue, or by sewing.

6. To turn this double ring into a tricorn, fold up three sides as shown. Use needle and thread to reinforce these folds: Starting from the inside of side A, push a needle to the outside at point 1.

Bring points 1 and 2 as close together as you can—even touching, if possible. Sew down through point 2 and back to point 1. Sew back and forth two or three more times until the hold is firm.

7. Repeat step 6 to bring side C up, using needle and thread to join it to side A at point 3 and to side B at point 4. Make corner 3-C as tight as possible; do the same with corner 4-C. Your tricorn is now ready to wear! If you want to add a crown, cut the visor off an old baseball cap; fit the cap inside the tricorn from underneath, and sew the bottom edge of the tricorn to the bottom edge of the cap.

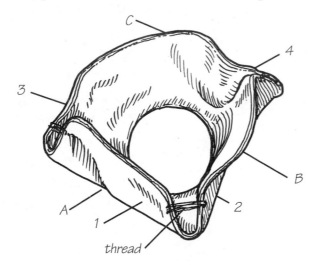

JEREMIAH'S RETURN

Nearly seven weeks after their father left for Boston, Laurie spotted him approaching along the river road and the whole Logan family rushed out to greet him. Jeremiah was exhausted from his travels, but eager to tell his news. The British had abandoned Boston, boarding their ships without firing a shot, and set sail for Canada. Word of Jeremiah's news spread rapidly and for the next week the Logans had visitors almost every day, all anxious to hear the details. The Virginia Patriots were thrilled by his report, but everyone knew the British would not give up. Jeremiah told them that General Washington was already marching his army toward New York City, where he expected the British to attack.

Because their mother was kept busy with the frequent visitors, Joshua and Laurie helped her with some of the cooking and baking. She showed them how to follow a recipe Jeremiah had brought from New England for a dessert called Indian pudding. They also made one of their father's favorites—cream scones.

CREAM SCONES

The majority of Americans in the 1770s traced their ancestry to Great Britain, so it was natural for them to follow many British customs, like serving afternoon tea. And with their tea (or coffee), both British and Americans enjoyed light foods, with scones being a favorite on both sides of the Atlantic. In this activity, you can make a batch of cream scones and serve them for a proper afternoon tea. Substitute milk or hot chocolate for the tea if you prefer. Scones make a tasty snack at any time, and you can serve them with breakfast or as a dessert.

INGREDIENTS

4 tablespoons soft butter (room temperature)
2 cups all-purpose flour
4 teaspoons sugar
2 teaspoons double-acting baking powder
½ teaspoon salt
2 eggs
½ cup light cream or whole milk
1 to 2 teaspoons water
butter, jam, or marmalade

EQUIPMENT

flour sifter
large mixing bowl
mixing spoon
fork
small mixing bowl
cup or small bowl
eggbeater or whisk
pastry cloth or clean countertop
rolling pin
sharp kitchen knife
cookie sheet
pastry brush
adult helper

MAKES

12 to 15 scones

1. Preheat the oven to 450 degrees F.

2. Sift the flour, 2 teaspoons of the sugar, the baking powder, and the salt into the large bowl. Save a tablespoon or two of the flour to use later. (You'll also have 2 teaspoons of sugar for later.) Stir with the mixing spoon.

3. Use a fork or your fingertips to work the butter, a little at a time, into the flour mixture.

4. Break the eggs into the small mixing bowl. Save about 2 tablespoons of the egg white in a cup or small bowl. (*Note:* Always wash your hands after handling raw eggs.)

5. Beat the eggs with the eggbeater or whisk and add to the flour mixture.

6. Stir in the cream or milk and continue stirring with the mixing spoon until the ingredients are blended. If the dough feels dry and crumbly, add a little more cream or milk.

7. Sprinkle the leftover flour onto a pastry cloth or clean countertop and turn the dough onto it. Knead the dough for no more than thirty seconds by working it with your fingers like a ball of clay.

8. Press the dough flat with the heels of your hands. Rub a little flour on the rolling pin and roll out the dough into a rectangle or oblong shape about ¾ inch thick. Place the dough on an ungreased cookie sheet.

9. Ask your adult helper to show you how to use a sharp kitchen knife to cut the dough into 12 to 15 squares. Or, for variety, make diagonal cuts for diamond-shaped scones.

10. Add a teaspoon or two of water to the egg white you saved. Dip a pastry brush into this, stir a little, then brush the egg white on the scones.

11. Sprinkle the remaining 2 teaspoons of sugar over the scones and bake for 15 minutes. The scones are done when the tops turn a light, golden brown. Serve warm with butter, jam, or marmalade.

 **NEW ENGLAND INDIAN PUDDING**

Early Americans ate lots of puddings because they were nourishing and provided an easy way to add some flavor to a diet that was usually bland. Puddings also kept well and, when firm, could be cut in slices and fried for breakfast. Indian pudding was a favorite dessert in New England from the 1600s on and soldiers carried the recipe to other parts of the country during the American Revolution. (Recipes in those days were called "receipts.")

The early New England settlers learned about corn from the Native Americans, and they probably would have been familiar with the Indians' slow-cooking pots of cornmeal, leading the settlers to use the name "Indian pudding" for several recipes, including the one you'll follow.

INGREDIENTS
5 cups milk
5 tablespoons yellow cornmeal
2 eggs
4 tablespoons butter
1 cup dark molasses
1 teaspoon cinnamon
1 teaspoon salt
vanilla ice cream or whipped cream

EQUIPMENT
double boiler with lid (or substitute a 2-quart
*   saucepan fit into a larger saucepan)*
small mixing bowl
eggbeater or whisk
mixing spoon
2-quart baking dish
adult helper

MAKES
6 to 8 servings

1. Fill the bottom half of the double boiler about ⅓ with water. (If you're using two saucepans, make sure the top saucepan fits into the larger one without forcing the water out.) Ask your adult helper to assist you with this and with heating the water to boiling.

2. While the water is heating, break the eggs into the bowl. Beat them well and set them aside. (Remember to wash your hands after handling the eggs.)

3. Pour 4 cups of the milk into the top of the double boiler. Heat it over the boiling water until little bubbles begin to form at the edges.

4. Slowly stir in the cornmeal, a little at a time. Cover the pan and lower the heat so that the water simmers. Cook the cornmeal over the hot water for 20 minutes, stirring occasionally. Check now and then to make sure the water has not cooked out of the bottom pan; add more water if necessary.

5. While the cornmeal is cooking, preheat the oven to 350 degrees F. Use 2 tablespoons of the butter to grease the bottom and sides of the baking dish.

6. After the cornmeal has cooked 20 minutes, remove the pan from the heat. Stir in the eggs, molasses, cinnamon, salt, and the remaining 2 tablespoons of butter. Continue stirring until the ingredients are blended.

7. Spoon the mixture into the buttered baking dish. Pour the remaining cup of cold milk on top and bake for one hour.

8. Have your adult helper remove the pudding from the oven. Let it stand for 20 to 30 minutes, then serve with a topping of vanilla ice cream or whipped cream.

Baking by Experience

In most American families of the late 1700s, the wife and mother managed the cooking and baking. Without modern appliances, or even an oven thermometer, she relied on experience and folk wisdom. The best oven of the time was only a brick-lined box built into the side of the fireplace. To start the baking, the cook made a fire in the oven, waited from one to three hours for the bricks to heat, then scraped out the ashes before putting in the items to be baked.

One way to measure the heat of the oven was to throw in a handful of flour; if the flour turned a burnt black instead of brown, the oven was too hot. Another hint was to twirl a wet broom inside the oven until it dried. This would prevent pies and cakes from being scorched on top.

CALM DAYS AND STORMY DAYS

Joshua was often so busy that he hardly thought about the war. In addition to his regular chores, he was now old enough to help his father work with the horses. The little strawberry roan became his special project, and by May, Patriot Lady, as he called her, was a fine saddle horse. On stormy days, Joshua worked with his father on indoor projects. They made wooden frames to fit around slate shingles so the children could use them with chalk for their lessons. They also used some scrap tin to make two lanterns, piercing holes in the sides in an eagle pattern.

Now and then the calm was shattered by a rider galloping into the farmyard to call Jeremiah for militia duty. Alarms were becoming frequent throughout the South because bands of Loyalists were forming regiments to fight the Patriots. So far, the Patriot militia had been well prepared and had won several skirmishes, although the Virginia town of Norfolk had been destroyed by fire. Joshua longed to be old enough to ride to battle with his father, but for now he had to be satisfied playing his

favorite strategy game with Laurie. Since the game was known by several names, they gave it a new one, calling it Patriots and Redcoats.

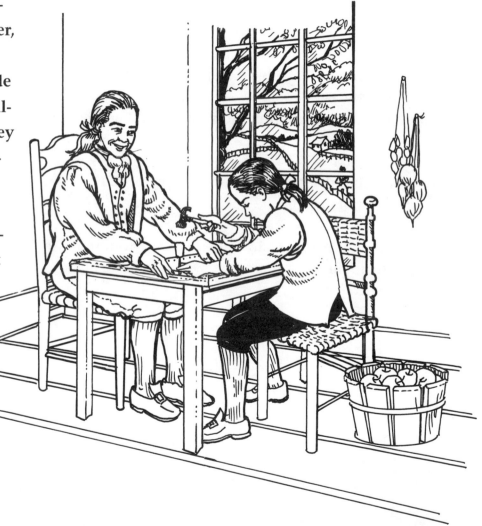

PROJECT THE GAME OF PATRIOTS AND REDCOATS

The American people believed in being practical and making good use of their time. They didn't like their children to waste time with toys and games unless the activity had some practical benefit. Several board games were popular, for example, because they could be used to teach basic elements of geography, history, or math. Others, like the ancient game of chess, were considered useful as ways of practicing military tactics and strategy.

The game you'll make and play is one variation of Fox and Geese, a strategy game that had been popular for several hundred years. The fact that one side was greatly outnumbered would have appealed to Patriot young people, because the Americans were outnumbered by the British in nearly every battle. In this game, the outnumbered side, with two game pieces, is the Patriots; the player with twenty-four game pieces represents the "Redcoats"—the Patriots' term for the red-coated British soldiers.

MATERIALS
several sheets of newspaper
white poster board, about 16 inches square
stiff cardboard, 16 inches square (optional)
scissors (optional)
white glue (optional)
ruler
pencil
black felt-tip pen, medium or fine point
1 package self-hardening clay (about 8 ounces needed)
sheet of wax paper
masking tape or transparent tape
table knife
acrylic paint or poster paint—blue, red, and other colors of your choice
small paintbrush
2 players

1. Spread the newspaper on your work surface and place the poster board on it. If the poster board doesn't lie perfectly flat, cut a piece of cardboard the same size and glue the poster board to it.

2. The game board is easy to lay out if you begin by using ruler and pencil to draw a rectangle measuring 12 inches by 4 inches across the middle of the poster board. Draw a second rectangle the same size going up and down the poster board, forming a large cross, as shown by the darker lines in the drawing.

3. Make a mark every 2 inches all the way around both rectangles. Be sure to mark the corners of each rectangle. You should have 33 marks.

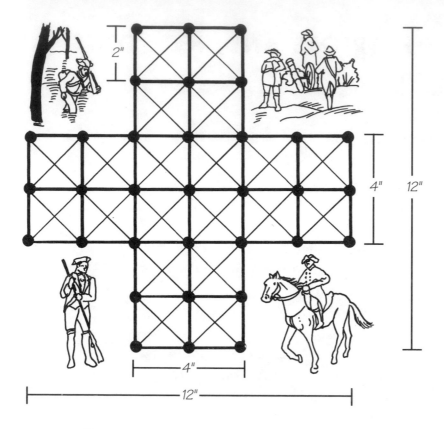

fortress. You can also draw battle pictures in the 4 corners outside the game board, as shown.

7. To make the game pieces, first tape a piece of wax paper to the newspaper. This will keep the newsprint from rubbing off on the clay.

8. Follow the directions on the package of clay for making the clay soft and workable, then roll out a large piece of clay into a cylinder 6½ inches long and ¾ inch in diameter.

9. With a table knife, cut the cylinder into 26 slices. These disks are your game pieces. Allow the clay to harden according to the directions on the package.

wax paper

¼"

¾"

4. Now connect all the dots. Your board will have 20 squares, each with an X inside, as indicated in the drawing.

5. With a black felt-tip pen, make all 33 marks a little larger and darker, as shown. These will be the 33 game spaces. Carefully go over all the lines with darker pencil lines, or with the pen, so they will stand out clearly.

6. With pencil, draw a barricade of logs or stones to set off 9 game spaces as the Patriots'

10. Paint 2 game pieces blue and 24 red. If you wish, paint the fortress and the corner pictures, too, using colors of your choice. Let the paint dry according to the directions on the bottle or tube. Your board and game pieces for Patriots and Redcoats are now ready.

Rules for Patriots and Redcoats

1. Use any method you wish to decide which player will be the Patriots and which the Redcoats.

2. Place the 24 Redcoats on the game board as indicated in the diagram. Put the 2 Patriot game pieces anywhere in the nine spaces of the fortress.

3. The object of the game: The Redcoats try to trap the Patriots, either in the fortress or anywhere on the game board battlefield, so they cannot move. The Redcoats can also win by occupying every space in the fortress. When the Patriot side can no longer make a move, or the fortress is occupied, he or she surrenders and the game is over.

The Patriots try to escape by capturing so many Redcoats that they can no longer be trapped. They capture a Redcoat by jumping the game piece, as in checkers. A Patriot can make as many jumps as possible, as long as there is a free space to land on, and the jumped Redcoats are removed from the board. The Redcoats *cannot* jump—either a Patriot or other Redcoats. The Redcoat player should surrender when he or she has only 4 or 5 game pieces left, since that isn't enough for trapping the Patriots.

4. The Patriots move first, one game piece in any direction on connecting lines to an empty space. Patriots must make a jump that is available, even if it puts the game piece in danger of being trapped.

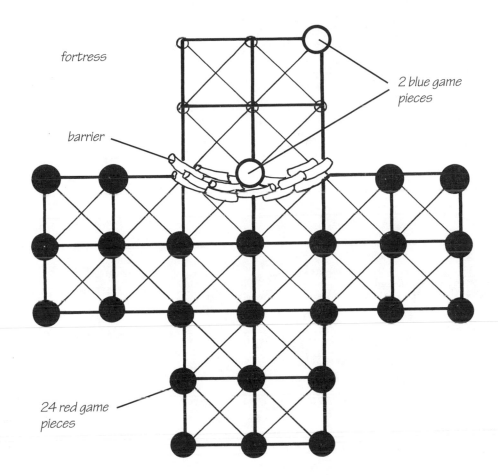

fortress

2 blue game pieces

barrier

24 red game pieces

5. The Redcoats can move in any direction *except* back. Remember that the Redcoats cannot capture a Patriot or jump any game piece.

6. Keep taking turns until one side is forced to surrender.

Patriots, Redcoats, and Others

Many men in Great Britain were unwilling to enlist as soldiers to fight in America, so King George III was forced to hire mercenaries—professional soldiers who would fight almost anywhere for money. More than 30,000 mercenaries fought for the British; since many came from the German state of Hesse, the Patriots called them all Hessians. The British also received strong support from American Loyalists.

The Patriots received outside help too, especially from France after that country joined the war in 1778. In fact, the Patriots might not have won without French supplies and weapons, as well as soldiers and a powerful navy. In addition, individual volunteers came from Poland, Germany, and other countries, because they believed in the cause of American independence.

Polish volunteer Thaddeus Kosciusko

 PROJECT PIERCED-TIN LANTERN

In the late 1700s, a century before the invention of electric lighting, people relied on a variety of slow-burning fuels to provide a little nighttime light. Substances like whale oil and fish oil were common, but wax candles were the major form of lighting, along with limited light from the fireplace. Holders for candles came in all sorts of sizes and shapes, from the single clay or metal candlestick to elaborate chandeliers that might hold thirty or more candles.

In this activity, you'll make a model of the pierced-tin lanterns that were popular at the time of the American Revolution. These lanterns, often carried on poles at night, gave people just enough light to guide them through the dark streets.

Caution: Making your lantern out of a juice can will give you a good idea of what piercing tin was like, but the piercing will leave sharp, jagged edges inside the lantern so you'll have to be careful not to reach inside. You and your adult helper may decide to substitute an aluminum foil oven liner (available in most supermarkets). Note the other substitute materials as well.

MATERIALS
several sheets of newspaper
large juice can with paper label, or substitute aluminum foil oven liner
    (foil baking pans are not quite as good because the piercing can produce
     jagged edges)
scrap paper
pencil
marking pen with permanent ink
water
2 old towels or clean rags

large nail
old screwdriver (not Phillips-head)
hammer
can opener
votive candle in glass container (available in most
    supermarkets)
adult helper
If using foil oven liner:
ruler
scissors
hole punch
2 short brass fasteners

1. Spread the newspaper over your work surface.

2. Remove the label from the juice can and make sure the inside is clean. One lid must remain on the can. For the foil oven liner, use scissors to cut a piece 8 inches wide and about 16 inches long.

3. Use scrap paper and pencil to plan your design. Use dots and dashes for the juice can, to correspond to piercing with a nail and a screwdriver; dots only for the foil. You can copy the designs shown here or create your own. Keep in mind that the more holes you make, the more the candlelight will show through.

4. Copy the design onto the can or foil with pencil, then go over it with marking pen so it

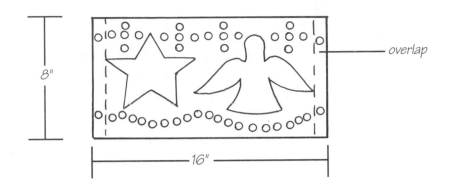

won't smudge (once the ink dries). If you're working with the foil, skip to step 9.

5. Fill the juice can with water and place it in the freezer for about 24 hours, or until it's frozen solid.

6. Fold a towel or rag in half and place it on your work surface. Lay the ice-filled can on its side on the towel. Have your adult helper work carefully but quickly to hammer the nail or the screwdriver through the dot-and-dash pattern on the can, hammering just hard enough to pierce the metal cleanly. Your helper should be able to finish while the ice keeps the surface firm for piercing.

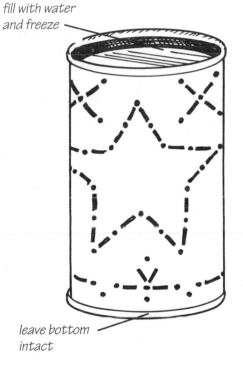

fill with water and freeze

leave bottom intact

7. When the piercing is finished, dump the ice and water into the sink. If the ice is still packed too tightly, let it thaw in the sink for a few minutes.

8. Cut the remaining lid off the can. Skip steps 9 and 10.

9. For the foil lantern, use the hole punch to go over your design. You'll notice that the foil doesn't create jagged edges.

10. Bend the foil into a cylinder shape; you may find it helpful to bend it around a can or bottle. Overlap the ends a little. Punch top and bottom holes through both layers, insert the brass fasteners, and bend back the prongs.

11. Ask your adult helper to light the candle. Carefully fit your lantern over the candle. Turn off other lights and enjoy the patterns created by your pierced tin.

PROJECT SCHOOL SLATE

Paper was costly in early America because machines had not been invented to produce it in large quantities. Hard work by hand was needed to turn rags or wood pulp into a mash that was then hand-pressed and dried to make each sheet. Instead of notebooks or pads, schoolchildren usually wrote their lessons with chalk on thin pieces of slate or wood. The slate was quite plentiful because it was used for roof shingles on churches and large houses. Instead of slate, you'll use materials that are available at most lumberyards and many hardware stores.

MATERIALS

several sheets of newspaper
1 piece of ¼-inch masonite, about 9 by 12 inches (lumberyards and hardware stores often sell scrap pieces or will cut the masonite for you)
sandpaper, medium or fine grit
damp paper towel
small can of blackboard paint (available wherever paint is sold)
paintbrush, 1 or 2 inches wide
white chalk
small clean rag or old washcloth

1. Spread the newspaper on your work surface.

2. Sand the edges of the masonite and round the corners a little. Do not sand the front or back of the masonite. Wipe off the sanding dust with a damp paper towel.

Hornbooks and Primers

There were few schools for American children in Revolutionary War days, except in New England, where the world's first public schools had been established. Books were also rare. While most families had a Bible, and perhaps a handful of books and an almanac, there weren't many books for children to learn from. One of the most common pieces of school equipment, both in New England's public schools and in the private schools scattered throughout the country, was the hornbook—a paddle-shaped piece of wood that held a printed sheet of paper (usually a page from the Bible) covered with a very thin sheet of horn to protect the page. A book called the *New England Primer* was also widely used. The *Primer* was filled with short moral tales and sayings, often from the Bible. More than 3 million had been printed by the 1770s.

3. Paint the smooth side of the masonite with 2 coats of the blackboard paint. Follow the directions on the can for drying times.

4. When the second coat of paint has dried, use a piece of white chalk to experiment with writing on your school slate. If the chalk doesn't show up well, erase the chalk with a clean rag or old washcloth, apply a third coat of paint, and let it dry. Now try writing some of your schoolwork on the slate. Imagine what it would be like to do all of your class work and homework on a slate!

CHAPTER TWO

SUMMER

The summer of 1776 began hopefully for the Patriots. In June, the Continental Congress began to debate the great issue of declaring independence. At the same time, Patriots in South Carolina defended the city of Charleston from attack by a British fleet, forcing the king's battered ships to sail away after a ferocious cannon battle. And, in Virginia, Jeremiah was with the militia when they defeated a Loyalist force of five hundred on the coast. But people's hopes were suddenly dashed by the frightening news that a huge British fleet of more than two hundred ships had sailed into New York harbor, ready to land an invasion force that would greatly outnumber the defenders commanded by Washington.

There was also trouble at home. Fierce summer storms struck while Joshua, his mother, and two neighbors frantically tried to cut and rake the Logans' hay crop. They could not work fast enough and half the crop rotted in the flooded fields.

A NEW NATION

One morning in July, the entire Logan family stopped what they were doing to watch a horse and rider coming toward them at full gallop. Whenever Jeremiah was away, the approach of a messenger raised fears that something had happened to him. But this messenger brought exciting news. Two weeks earlier, on July 4, 1776, the Congress had approved the Declaration of Independence. The thirteen British colonies had now become the thirteen states of America. The messenger also reported that Jeremiah was safe and the militia were on the way home. Soon after the men returned, there was to be an Independence celebration.

During the days that heavy rain kept the family indoors, Frances Logan had time to help the children with new lessons and new projects. They used clay from their creek bed to make models of Philadelphia's Liberty Bell and they made several small rugs by painting stenciled designs on pieces of canvas. They also used scraps of canvas and paint to make their own version of a flag for their new nation.

PROJECT STARS AND STRIPES FLAG

The Revolutionary War was a period of wonderful creativity in flag making, especially after independence was declared. Patriot men and women designed new flags for each of the thirteen states and for the nation, and that was only the beginning. Every regiment in the Continental Army and in each state's militia had its own regimental flag. Many generals and sea captains designed their own flags, and there were even flags for particular battles.

When the thirteen colonies united to fight Great Britain in 1775, the "Grand Union Flag" became the first national flag, although it still displayed the British Union Jack in the upper left corner. Following the Declaration of Independence, the first stars and stripes flag appeared. In 1777 the stars were arranged in a circle and this design remained in use until 1818, even after two new states led to 15 stars and 15 stripes. Every flag was sewn by hand, of course, but in this activity you'll use felt and glue instead of needle and thread.

(**Note:** Felt is recommended because the seams won't unravel and glue is less likely to "bleed" through the fabric. However, with care, you can substitute heavy cotton if felt is not available.)

MATERIALS

several sheets of newspaper
piece of white felt, about 15 inches by 20 inches
ruler
pencil
scissors
piece of blue felt, about 8 inches square
scrap of paper
piece of red felt, about 8 inches by 20 inches
fabric glue, craft glue, or white glue
thumbtacks, pushpins, or tape for hanging

1. Spread the newspaper on your work surface and place the piece of white felt on it.

2. With ruler and pencil, draw a rectangle measuring 13 inches by 19 inches. Cut out the rectangle and save the scraps of fabric.

3. Measure and cut a 7-inch square of the blue felt. Spread thin threads of glue on the back, or "wrong" side, of the fabric and press it on the front, or "right" side, of the white rectangle in the upper left corner, as shown.

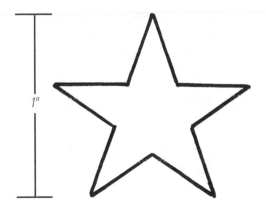

1"

The Legend of Betsy Ross

In 1776, a widow named Elizabeth "Betsy" Ross received a visit from General Washington at her home in Philadelphia. According to her grandson, recalling the incident many years later, Mrs. Ross and the general talked about designing a flag for the new nation. They made several sketches and Mrs. Ross, a well-known seamstress, said, "I will try to make it."

Did Betsy Ross design and sew the first Stars and Stripes flag? Many people think so. But others say that the only evidence is the story told in later years by her grandson who was only five years old at the time of the visit, plus mention of it in a few family letters. Until more facts are discovered, historians say, the story is a legend, not a fact.

4. On a scrap of paper, copy or trace the pattern for the star. Cut out the paper pattern and place it on a scrap of white felt. Trace around the pattern with pencil and cut out the star. Use the pattern to make 12 more white stars.

5. Before gluing the stars, position them on the blue square in the arrangement shown—three rows of three stars and two rows of two. Glue one star at a time, spreading a very thin line of glue on the back so that each point of the star has a little glue. Carefully press the star in place and go on to the next one.

6. Carefully measure and cut three strips of red felt, 1 inch wide and 19 inches long. Glue these to the bottom part of the flag. Make sure that there are 1-inch white strips in between the red and that one red strip runs along the bottom border.

7. Measure and cut four red strips 1 inch wide and 12 inches long. Glue one of these strips along the top edge of the flag and a second strip that extends from the bottom of the blue square to the right edge of the flag. Glue the last two red strips in place, with 1-inch white stripes in between. Your replica of the first Stars and Stripes is finished. Display it proudly on the wall of your room with thumbtacks, pushpins, or tape.

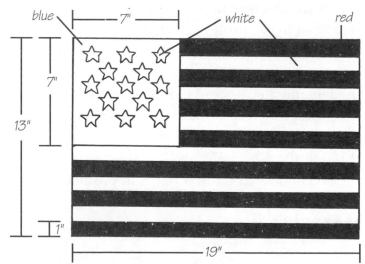

The Liberty Bell in Philadelphia is one of the most famous symbols of American freedom and democracy. It became associated with the Declaration of Independence when it was rung on July 8, 1776 (not July 4), to announce the first public reading of the document. For your model of the Liberty Bell, you can use either self-hardening clay or regular modeling clay. Regular modeling clay is a little more flexible than the self-hardening, and it usually costs less; in this project, you can also let it air dry rather than having it "fired" in a kiln (a special oven for finishing ceramic items).

MATERIALS

several sheets of newspaper
piece of masonite or plywood about 14 by 24 inches
plastic or pottery flowerpot, 6 or 7 inches high, about
   5¼ inches in diameter at the top, tapering to about
   3¼ inches at the bottom
sheet of aluminum foil, about 10 inches
scissors
2 pounds of clay, modeling or self-hardening
table knife
craft stick or modeling tools for clay
small bowl of water
piece of sponge
pencil

1 or 2 sheets of paper
tempera or acrylic paints—white, orange, blue, red,
   green, yellow, purple
small paintbrush
black felt-tip pen, fine point

1. Spread the newspaper on your work surface and place the masonite or plywood on top. This makes a good surface for working with clay.

2. Cover the flowerpot with aluminum foil, pressing the foil around the lip of the pot to hold it in place. The foil will make it easier to remove the pot later.

3. Place the clay on the masonite and flatten it by pounding it and pressing it with the heels of your hands. Continue pushing the clay down and working it with your fingers to make a round, flat disk—like a dinner plate or a pancake—about ¼ inch thick.

4. Position the flattened clay over the upside-down flowerpot and press it down the sides. The clay will bunch up in some places or split in others as you press it into the flowerpot shape, but you can easily smooth out those places with a table knife and craft stick or modeling tools.

5. Put more clay at the top and round it into the bell shape. Form a small piece of clay into a wide U shape and fix it to the top of the bell by moistening the clay with a little water. (It's best not to use this piece as a handle for lifting or carrying the bell.)

6. Work some clay into a thin, flat rope and fit it around the base of your model to shape the lower part of the bell.

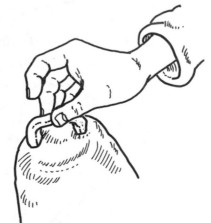

7. Go over the entire surface of the model with your fingers and modeling tools to make it as smooth as possible. Dampen a piece of sponge and use that to create an even smoother finish.

8. Allow the clay to dry for 2 or 3 days before painting it. (If you're using self-hardening clay, follow the directions for drying on the package.) When the clay is nearly dry, you can remove the flowerpot and foil, or you can leave the flowerpot in to give the model greater weight if you prefer.

9. Like old statues and roofing made of copper, the bell weathered from its original penny color to an attractive gray tinged with green. Before trying to reproduce that color, prepare your model by applying an undercoat of white paint—unless the clay you worked with is already a very light color.

10. While the undercoat dries, draw three rough bell shapes on a sheet of paper. Mix blue paint with orange to create a shade of gray and apply this to one of the drawings. Next, mix red and green to create a different gray for a second drawn bell, then purple and yellow for the third. Choose the gray you like best and apply two coats of it to your model. Follow directions on the paint bottle or tube for drying time between coats. After applying the second coat, you can try adding just a touch of green while the paint is wet.

11. When the paint is dry, use a pencil to draw the lines that go all the way around the bell, as shown in the picture. Correct any mistakes in the lines, then go over them carefully with the felt-tip pen.

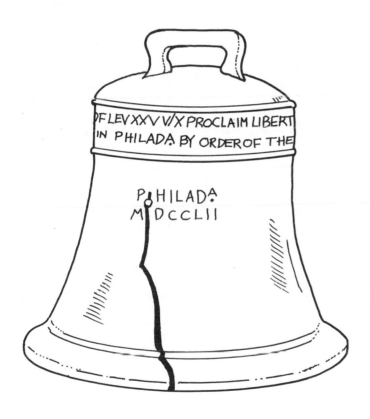

12. On the top line, write the lines from the Bible first in pencil, then in pen. Study the picture to see which words appear on the crack side of the bell. (If you find the lettering is too difficult, try printing only the words that are on the same side as the crack.)

Here is the quotation (from the Book of Leviticus, 25:10):

PROCLAIM LIBERTY THROUGHOUT THE LAND UNTO ALL THE INHABITANTS THEREOF LEV XXV V/X

13. If you can manage the printing, add the next line of writing on the bell:

BY ORDER OF THE PENNSYLVANIA PROVINCIAL ASSEMBLY, THE STATE HOUSE IN PHILADA

If this much printing is too difficult, you can either leave this line out or print only the words on the side where the crack is. Add the name of the company that made the bell: PASS AND STOW, and the year: MDCCLII. When you're satisfied with the lettering, go over everything with the pen.

14. Finally, draw the crack in pencil and fill it in with pen. Your model Liberty Bell is now ready for you to display, to give as a gift, or to use as a paperweight.

Biography of the Bell

The 2,000-pound Liberty Bell was cast in 1751 to celebrate the fiftieth anniversary of a new constitution for Pennsylvania. The bell first cracked about a year later and had to be re-cast. Late in 1776, when the British were approaching Philadelphia, the bell was moved to Allentown, where it was hidden until the British left.

After the Revolution, the bell remained in service for many years. According to legend, it cracked again in 1835, during the funeral of John Marshall, Chief Justice of the Supreme Court, and again in 1846, while honoring the anniversary of George Washington's birth. It did not become known as the Liberty Bell until 1839, early in the movement to abolish slavery in America. The bell remained in Philadelphia's Independence Hall until 1976, when it was moved about 100 yards to a special pavilion.

PROJECT STENCILED FLOORCLOTH

In the mid-1700s, wealthy Americans began to import beautiful wool rugs from parts of Asia called the Orient. Most families could not afford these colorful floor coverings, which are still known as Oriental rugs, but they soon found ways to make good imitations by painting designs on canvas. Some tried to copy the geometric designs of the Oriental rugs, while others preferred to paint scenes. The use of stencils for the designs became popular in the 1770s and stenciled floorcloths were widely used until the late 1800s.

For your stenciled floorcloth, you'll use the same techniques Americans used in Revolutionary War times. You can buy inexpensive lightweight canvas at most discount department stores and also at paint stores. Artist's canvas is not recommended because it is much more expensive. If necessary, you can substitute denim, kettlecloth, or other heavy cotton fabric.

MATERIALS
piece of canvas or other heavy cotton cloth, 36 by 18 inches
electric iron
several sheets of newspaper
1 pint latex wall paint—white, off-white, or light tan
sponge brush, 2 to 3 inches wide
pencil
ruler
2 pieces of thin cardboard, such as poster board or file folders, 4 by 6 inches
scissors
old magazine or cutting board
craft knife
masking tape

acrylic paint—brown, red, and green
3 paper cups
stencil brush, or small brush with stiff bristles
paper towels
scrap paper
piece of sponge (natural sponge if possible)
red permanent marking pen
acrylic varnish or sealer, or polyurethane
piece of plastic wrap
adult helper

1. With an adult's help, iron the canvas to remove wrinkles.

2. Spread the newspaper on your work surface or on the floor, with the canvas spread flat on it. Use the sponge brush to apply two coats of the latex wall paint. Allow an hour drying time after each coat, then apply a single coat on the back of the canvas. Clean the sponge brush right away in warm, soapy water.

3. Use the paint drying time to prepare your stencils. Draw a stencil design on each piece of cardboard; positioning the drawing in the middle of the 4-by-6-inch card, as shown. Either copy the designs shown here or create your own. (If you make your own stencil design, keep it simple. Remember that the bridges—the parts that connect the cut-away portions—are *not* the parts that show when painted.)

4. Place one of the stencil cards on a magazine or cutting board. Ask your adult helper to use the craft knife to cut out the stencil. Any mistakes can be covered up with masking tape. Repeat for the second stencil.

5. With ruler and pencil (or one of the stencil cards) make a pencil mark every 6 inches, all the way around the canvas, about 2 inches in from the edge of the canvas.

6. Position the apple stencil in between the first and second pencil marks, as shown in the drawing. Hold the stencil in place with small pieces of masking tape. You can cover the apple stem and leaf with masking tape, too, so that you don't accidentally paint them red.

7. Pour a little red paint into a paper cup. Hold the stencil brush in a vertical position (straight up and down) and dip it lightly into the paint. To avoid overloading the brush, tap it on a paper towel to remove the excess.

8. Paint the first apple by sweeping the brush from the stencil card toward the middle of the stencil opening, as shown.

pencil marks

tape

2"

2"

6"

6"

9. Allow the paint to dry for 2 or 3 minutes, then carefully lift the stencil straight up and off. (If it takes more than 3 minutes for the paint to dry, you've probably used too much paint.)

10. Move the stencil to the space between your third and fourth pencil marks. Repeat steps 8 and 9 for this second apple, then continue all the way around the canvas, always skipping a 6-inch space for the tree trunk stencil.

11. Rinse out the brush, take the tape off the apple stem, and reposition the stencil over the first apple. Pour a little brown paint in a cup, and paint the apple stem. You can continue all the way around and finish the stems, or you can stencil a tree trunk while each apple stem dries.

12. Follow the same technique for stenciling the apple leaves. Clean the brush in soapy water.

13. For the tops of the trees, dampen the piece of sponge with a little water, dip it into the green paint, and practice dabbing it on a piece of scrap paper. When you're satisfied with how your sponged treetops look, paint all the treetops on your floorcloth.

14. When the paint is dry, use the red marking pen to add a few apple-like dots to each of the trees.

15. To finish your floorcloth, use the sponge brush to apply two coats of acrylic varnish or sealer, or polyurethane. If possible, apply these finishes outdoors to speed the drying time and reduce odor or fumes. (*Note:* Acrylic varnish is safe to use, but spray cans are not recommended.) Between coats, wrap the brush in plastic wrap,

airtight. Follow the directions on the container for drying times. These finishing coats will keep the edges from unraveling and will provide good protection for your floorcloth. Dirt or spots can be cleaned up with a rag and soapy water.

16. Your stenciled floorcloth is now ready to use, maybe as a rug by your bed or study area. For storage, roll up the rug with the paint side out; do not fold.

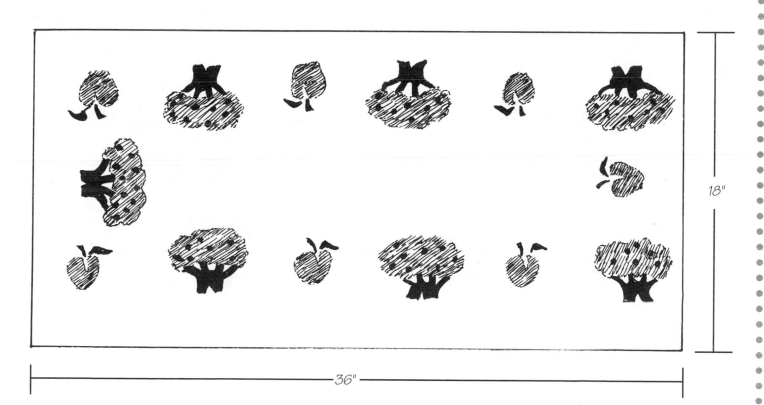

36"

18"

THE FIRST INDEPENDENCE DAY

News traveled slowly in 1776, so people in outlying regions did not learn of the Declaration of Independence until several weeks after July Fourth. As a result, celebrations of this first Independence Day took place at different times throughout the summer.

In the foothills of the Blue Ridge Mountains, the Logans and their friends had a special reason to celebrate. They had learned that one of the men who actually wrote the great document was their neighbor—Thomas Jefferson. Jefferson was a plantation owner who was building a grand house on the hills overlooking Charlottesville.

The celebration began with a public reading of the Declaration, which was greeted by cheers and applause. Although ammunition was in short supply, the militiamen fired rifles, muskets, and several small cannons. The rest of the day

was spent visiting with friends and sharing an enormous picnic. Joshua and Laurie had helped their mother prepare for the feast. Laurie used dried strawberries and fresh blueberries to make what they called their "Independence Day shortcake," Joshua made nut sweetmeats, and all the children helped pick the blueberries.

PROJECT NUT SWEETMEATS

Although Americans in the 1700s were fond of sweets, most forms of modern candy were unknown to them. They did make a variety of what they called "sweetmeats" out of molasses, maple syrup, and sometimes sugar. Sugar and chocolate, however, were expensive commodities that had to be imported, so the modest amounts most families could afford were used for baking rather than candy.

INGREDIENTS

2 cups maple sugar or brown sugar
¼ cup water
1 tablespoon butter
1 cup chopped or broken walnuts

EQUIPMENT

medium saucepan
mixing spoon
candy thermometer or cup of cold water
wax paper
adult helper

MAKES

about 8 snack servings

1. Mix the sugar, water, and butter together in the saucepan.

2. Have your adult helper cook the mixture over low heat for about 15 to 20 minutes, until the temperature on a candy thermometer reaches 238 degrees F or a small amount dropped into a cup of cold water forms a soft ball.

3. Add the nuts.

4. Remove from heat and stir until the mixture is thickened.

5. Drop spoonsful of the mixture onto wax paper. The mixture will spread a little, so don't put the spoonsful too close together. Let the candies harden.

 **INDEPENDENCE DAY SHORTCAKE**

Americans in the 1700s used a variety of berries to make a dessert much like modern strawberry shortcake. From late spring through the autumn, one variety of wild berry after another was ready for picking, beginning with strawberries in June and ending with raspberries into October. The berries were served on pieces of bread and topped with heavy cream. By the mid-1700s, this "fruit bread" was being changed to a fruit shortcake, with a biscuit dough replacing bread. You'll find that this recipe is quick and easy, and it makes a colorful dessert for Fourth of July celebrations.

INGREDIENTS

1 pint strawberries
1 pint blueberries
5 tablespoons sugar
1¾ cups all-purpose flour
2½ teaspoons double-acting baking powder
1¼ teaspoons salt
⅛ cup vegetable shortening
¾ cup milk or cream
about 2 tablespoons butter (¼ stick)
can of ready-to-use whipped cream or 1 pint heavy cream

EQUIPMENT

fruit huller
colander
paring knife
medium-size mixing bowl
sifter
large mixing bowl
mixing spoon
fork
breadboard or clean counter
round biscuit cutter, or glass 3 inches in diameter
piece of wax paper
cookie sheet
pastry brush
table knife
oven mitts
4 to 5 dessert plates
adult helper

MAKES

4 to 6 dessert servings

1. Preheat the oven to 450 degrees F.

2. Hull the strawberries and wash them in the colander. With an adult's help, use a paring knife to cut the strawberries into large chunks and place them in the medium mixing bowl. Save at least 6 whole berries for decoration.

3. Wash the blueberries in the colander and place them in the mixing bowl with the strawberries. (Save some for decoration.) Sprinkle about 4 tablespoons of sugar over the berries, and set the bowl aside.

4. Sift the flour, baking powder, salt, and 1 tablespoon of sugar into the large mixing bowl. Stir well with a large spoon.

5. Stir in the shortening with a fork. Continue to work the fork through the mixture until it is crumbly—like dry cornmeal or uncooked cream of wheat.

6. Pour in the milk or cream and stir well—or mix with your fingers—until the ingredients are blended into a soft dough.

7. Form the dough into a ball and place it on a lightly floured board or countertop. Knead the dough lightly with your fingertips for no more than 30 seconds, folding it over on itself two or three times.

8. Sprinkle a little flour on your hands and pat the dough into a circle about 1 inch thick.

9. Cut the dough in circles with a biscuit cutter or a glass. Press straight down when you're cutting; don't twist the cutter or the dough will stick to it.

10. After you've cut 3 or 4 biscuits, scrape the remaining dough together, form it into a ball, press flat, and cut again. You should have a total of 4 to 6 biscuits.

11. Use a piece of wax paper to spread a very little butter on the cookie sheet to grease it lightly.

12. Place the biscuits on the cookie sheet. Use a pastry brush to brush a little butter or milk on top of the biscuits to brown them.

13. Place the cookie sheet in the oven and bake for 12 to 15 minutes, until the biscuits are golden brown on top and feel firm to the touch.

14. Ask your adult helper to remove the cookie sheet from the oven. While the biscuits are still warm, cut them in half with a table knife and spread a little butter on both halves.

15. Place two biscuit halves on each dessert plate. Spoon strawberries and blueberries over both halves. Swirl whipped cream or cream over the berries, then decorate with the saved berries. Your patriotic red, white, and blue Independence Day shortcake is now ready to serve.

JOSHUA'S FIRST JOURNEY

In September, Joshua made his first trading trip with his father—a seventy-mile journey to Richmond to trade horses for grain that would help make up for the hay the Logans had lost. The journey took three days each way, with Joshua driving the wagon while his father led the horses.

They slept on the ground at night until they reached Richmond, where they spent the night at an inn. This made Joshua feel very grown-up—except that he was suffering with a sore throat. After dinner at the inn, they went outside to watch four Continental soldiers play a game of ninepins, rolling a ball down a long board to knock over the pins. The soldiers told them that the war news was not good. The British invasion of New York City had begun and Washington's forces were retreating. Although the soldiers said the city would not fall to the British, Joshua could tell that his father was worried.

Later in the evening, the innkeeper showed them a model of a battle scene he was making out of wood. The miniature ships and men were in a three-sided box, with background scenes painted on the sides. Before they left the next morning, the innkeeper's wife gave

Joshua a syrup of horseradish and sugar for his sore throat. It tasted awful but seemed to relieve the soreness. On the way home, Joshua decided he would learn to play ninepins and would make a model scene, but he was not so sure about the sore throat remedy.

PROJECT HOME REMEDIES

There were few trained doctors in the 1700s and even they knew very little about the causes and cures of illness. Most families relied on folk medicine—simple home remedies that worked well enough to be handed down from one generation to the next. Many remedies relied on common household items, such as vinegar, honey, and salt. Others were made of various herbs and other plants. Some of the most effective herbal remedies had been learned from Native American healers. Some of these tribal healers acted as unofficial community doctors in frontier regions.

This activity offers a sampling of home remedies for you to try. Most of these recipes are helpful and you can have fun trying them out. Keep in mind, however, that these ideas are not offered as cures for any ailment or condition. And, in case of allergies, always check with an adult before you try any folk formula.

Oatmeal Scrub

This is a gentle cleanser that will leave your skin feeling soft as well as clean.

MATERIALS

½ cup uncooked old-fashioned oatmeal (not the quick-cooking or instant kind)

washcloth

1. Place the uncooked oatmeal in the middle of the washcloth and fold over the corners.

2. Keep the washcloth folded so the oats don't fall out. Dampen the cloth with plenty of water and rub it over your skin in the bathtub or shower, or when you're washing your face.

3. Repeat daily for five or six days and feel the difference.

Homemade Toothpaste

Although the toothbrush was not invented until the 1790s, people used clean rags and various formulas to keep their teeth clean and their breath pleasant. A favorite tooth cleaner in early summer was nothing more than a fresh strawberry rubbed on the teeth and gums. The recipe you'll try includes bicarbonate of soda, which is used in several modern toothpastes.

INGREDIENTS

1 tablespoon salt

3 tablespoons bicarbonate of soda

2 teaspoons glycerine (available at most drugstores and many supermarkets)

water

a few drops of peppermint oil (available in the baking
section of supermarkets)

EQUIPMENT
small bowl
spoon
toothbrush or clean cloth

1. Mix the salt and bicarbonate of soda together in a small bowl. Stir in the glycerine.

2. Add just enough water to make a paste. Stir well.

3. Stir in a few drops of peppermint oil for flavor.

4. Use as you would regular toothpaste, either on a toothbrush or on a clean cloth, as people did in 1776.

Cough Syrup

While this formula is not a cure for a cough, a cold, or anything else, it makes a soothing syrup that usually will reduce coughing and soothe a sore throat. The same ingredients are found in modern honey-lemon cough drops.

INGREDIENTS
water
1 lemon
2 tablespoons glycerine
2 tablespoons honey

EQUIPMENT
small saucepan
paring knife
spoon
juice squeezer
cup, small jar, or small bowl
adult helper

1. Fill the saucepan half-full with water, place the lemon in it, and bring the water to a boil. Ask your adult helper to cook the lemon gently for about 10 minutes.

2. With the adult's help, rinse the lemon in cool water. When the lemon is cool enough to handle, have the adult cut it in half.

3. With your hand or a juice squeezer, squeeze the juice into a cup or small jar.

4. Add the glycerine and honey. Stir well to mix the ingredients thoroughly.

5. Take 1 teaspoonful as needed to ease the cough. You can also make slightly larger quantities to store in a covered jar for several days.

Balm for Chapped Lips

This simple remedy soothes chapped lips and helps keep them moist.

INGREDIENTS

½ teaspoon rose water (available at most drugstores and supermarkets)
2 tablespoons honey

EQUIPMENT

cup
spoon

1. Stir the rose water and honey together in a cup.

2. Apply a small amount to chapped lips with the tip of your finger. Repeat every hour as needed.

Remedies to Avoid

Most of the home remedies people relied on either helped the patient or at least didn't cause any harm. But, since no one yet knew what caused diseases or infections, doctors and others sometimes resorted to some strange cures. One remedy for a severe fever, for example, called for paring the patient's nails, placing the parings in a linen bag, then tying the bag around the neck of an eel. The eel would swim away and the patient would be cured! Another remedy, for a wide range of ailments from coughs to broken bones, called for formulas that included ground-up earthworms.

Perhaps the most dangerous remedy was the practice of bloodletting. The idea was to remove bad "humors" by drawing off blood, either with a sharp instrument called a lancet or by applying leeches. Even the leading Americam physician of the time, Dr. Benjamin Rush of Philadelphia, was a strong believer in bleeding. If enough blood was drawn off, of course, the patient became too weak to recover.

PROJECT A DIORAMA

Long before the invention of modern forms of entertainment, such as television and movies, people still enjoyed pictures that told a story. One popular form of entertainment developed in the 1700s was called a panorama. This was a scene—or a series of scenes—painted on a long piece of canvas attached to two rolls; as the rolls were turned, new parts of the picture emerged as others disappeared on the take-up roll. Even more popular was the form that later became known as a diorama. A diorama is created by placing objects in a box that has background scenes painted on the sides, producing a three-dimensional picture. Dioramas are still widely used today for such things as historical displays and museum exhibits.

For your diorama, use a shoe box or even something a little smaller. You can copy the hilly farm scene pictured here, or create your own historical scene.

MATERIALS

shoe box or sturdy gift box
several sheets of paper for drawing and painting
pencil
ruler
scissors
several sheets of newspaper
poster paints or acrylic paints
small brush
craft glue or white glue
package (1 pound) self-hardening clay—white, if possible
twigs for trees
moss for grass
toothpicks for fences
small stones for rocks and boulders
blue construction paper for a pond or stream
large piece of clear plastic wrap
transparent tape

Hints: Here are two helpful ideas for making dioramas:
• Rather than paint background scenes on the box itself, cut pieces of paper to fit the three sides and bottom of the diorama. Draw and paint your scenes on the paper, then glue the completed pictures to the box, as shown.
• You can make houses, barns, and other structures out of small boxes or pieces of cardboard, but it's usually easier to paint these on the side or back panels of the diorama.

1. Turn the box on its side so that the open top is facing you. The side of the box resting on your work surface will now be the bottom of the diorama.

2. Decide what you want to include in your diorama—what will be on the background scenes and what will be solid objects. You might find it useful to make a rough sketch of what goes where.

3. With ruler and pencil, measure pieces of paper to fit the three sides and bottom of the diorama. Cut out the pieces and write lightly in pencil where each will go—left panel, back panel, and so on.

4. Draw your scenes for the side and back panels, saving the bottom until these are finished. Keep in mind that objects that are far away, such as hills, trees, and buildings, should be drawn smaller than objects that are close. Remember also that your scenes wrap around. That is, a hill on the left panel can continue on the back panel.

5. After drawing the 3 pictures, spread newspaper over your work surface, and use poster paints or acrylics to fill the pictures in.

6. When the paint is dry (about 10 minutes), spread a little glue on the back of each panel and attach all three to the box.

7. For the bottom of the diorama, you might want to paint a single color—green for a summer scene, a sandy brown for autumn or early spring, white for winter. You might also want to include

a stream, path, or road that runs from one of the panels to the front of the diorama. Once you've decided, paint the bottom piece, let the paint dry, then glue it in place.

8. Use small pieces of clay to shape people, animals, low hills, or any other objects you want to include.

9. If you use twigs for trees, you can leave the "branches" bare, or cut and paint green paper tops to glue on the trees. Stick the base of each tree into a low mound of clay to hold it up.

10. If you're making a farm fence, it's best to construct it one section at a time—two upright posts and two cross pieces. Lay the pieces flat to glue them. Make a clay base on the bottom of the diorama and assemble the fence by sticking each section into the clay. Paint each clay base the same color as the bottom of the diorama.

11. Shape a piece of blue construction paper for a pond or stream, glue it to the bottom of the box. For the sparkling effect of sun on water, glue plastic wrap over the blue paper.

12. Paint all of the objects that require it before you put them in the diorama. When the paint is dry, arrange all objects in the diorama. Make any adjustments you want in the positions, then glue each object in place, including the low clay mounds that you're using to hold other objects.

13. Cut a piece of clear plastic wrap about 1 inch larger than the box opening. Attach it to the box with transparent tape and your diorama is ready to display.

CHAPTER THREE

AUTUMN

Autumn was a busy season for the Wentworths' lodging house in Philadelphia. Many of their lodgers were merchants who were arranging shipments of grain from Pennsylvania farms to eastern cities. Others had business with the Continental Congress, which met in the State House, just two streets away.

When twelve-year-old Peggy Wentworth was helping out in the parlor or the dining room, she often heard the lodgers talking in low, serious tones. In the autumn of 1776, the topic was always the same: the British had captured New York City and there was little left of the Continental Army. Some lodgers said the Patriot cause was now hopeless; others argued that as long as Washington could keep an army together, there was hope. Peggy knew that her parents wished the Patriots would give up and make peace but, as innkeepers, they did not want to offend their guests by speaking out.

UNCERTAIN TIMES

Nearly all of the Wentworths' lodgers were Patriots, and Peggy could tell that their mood was growing gloomier every day. They knew that Washington was leading the ragged remnants of his army across New Jersey, and they guessed that he hoped to reach Pennsylvania. Once there, the Delaware River would form a good defensive barrier, giving him time to rebuild his army and hope more militia would come.

Peggy admired the way her father could take part in the discussions without taking sides. He explained to her that innkeepers should be good hosts to all visitors. Peggy liked that idea and made up her mind not to show how worried she was about the Continental soldiers and the great General Washington. She pleased her mother by working extra hard and asking to help more in the kitchen. Peggy enjoyed cooking and her mother encouraged her to try different recipes, like one for spiced acorn squash. Her mother also made sure that she kept up with her reading, penmanship, and sewing. Together they had finished the squares for a quilt and Peggy decided to use the pattern to make a fancy bookmark.

QUILT PATTERN BOOKMARK

Every piece of cloth was slowly made by hand so people were careful not to waste it. Even worn-out clothing was cut into small pieces for making quilts. Quilt making itself gradually became one of America's foremost craft forms. Women—and some men—developed remarkable artistry in creating beautiful designs that were often very complex. A well-made quilt became a family heirloom, treasured by each generation, and some are still preserved today in art and craft museums throughout the country.

In this activity, you'll use contruction paper in different colors to reproduce a quilt pattern for a bookmark. Although you won't be hand-stitching every piece, you'll get a good idea of the care and precision needed to cut, sort, and assemble the many parts of a single quilt square.

MATERIALS

several sheets of newspaper
scraps, or small pieces, of construction paper, 1 dark
   color and several lighter ones
scrap of paper
scrap of poster board or thin cardboard
ruler
pencil
scissors

piece of poster board, white or any light shade,
   3¼ inches by 6½ inches
craft glue or white glue
ballpoint pen or fountain pen, black ink (optional)
clear plastic wrap, about 8 inches
transparent tape

1. Spread the newspaper on your work surface and place the pieces of construction paper on top.

2. Your first task is to decide on a color scheme. You can see that the pattern, called "Building Blocks," is an optical illusion; that is, if you look at it from different angles or upside down, the pattern looks quite different. You can also see that the design is made up of seven blocks, and each block has three diamond-shaped pieces, or faces. The optical illusion will work best if one of the faces in each block (labeled A) is a dark color, such as dark blue, dark green, or even black. The other faces can be any color, but you may find it easier to fit the pieces together if all the faces shown with dots (labeled B) are one color, like a light yellow, beige, or any other shade that goes well with the dark piece. The seven faces labeled C can be all different colors.

3. Carefully trace the diamond-shaped pattern (labeled "template") onto a piece of scrap paper and cut it out with scissors. Lay the paper cut-out pattern over the drawing in the book to make sure they are exactly the same. If the pattern you cut out isn't quite right, it's best to do it over or all seven blocks may be mismatched.

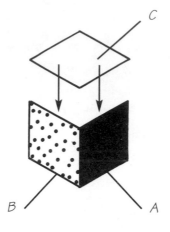

4. Place the paper pattern on a scrap of poster board or thin cardboard, trace around it with pencil, and cut it out. Again, check to be certain it matches the pattern in the book. This poster board diamond will make a sturdy template for measuring all 21 pieces in your design.

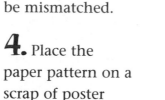

5. Use the template to trace and cut out 7 pieces of the dark color (A). Remember to trace and cut carefully so that the pieces will fit together.

6. Set the color A faces aside and repeat step 5 for seven B faces and then the seven C colors.

7. Decide where on your 3¼- by 6½-inch-long bookmark you want to place the pattern. Carefully position one A-B-C block on the poster board—but don't glue the pieces yet. If you like the way the arrangement looks, position the other six blocks, still not glued, around the first.

8. Begin gluing at the bottom left corner and fix the first 3-piece block to the bookmark. Carefully glue the rest of the pieces in place, working from the bottom of the bookmark to the top so that you don't accidentally move the unglued pieces.

9. When all the pieces are in place, you can add your name to the bookmark with ballpoint pen or fountain pen, if you wish. Or, if you're giving it as a gift, write the person's name and any greeting.

10. Cut a piece of clear plastic wrap a little wider than the pattern and long enough to wrap around to the back of the bookmark.

11. Stretch the plastic wrap as smoothly as you can and use pieces of transparent tape to fix it to the back of the bookmark. Place two longer pieces of tape across the front of the bookmark, one to seal the top of the plastic wrap, the other to seal the bottom. Your quilt pattern bookmark is now ready to use or to give as a gift.

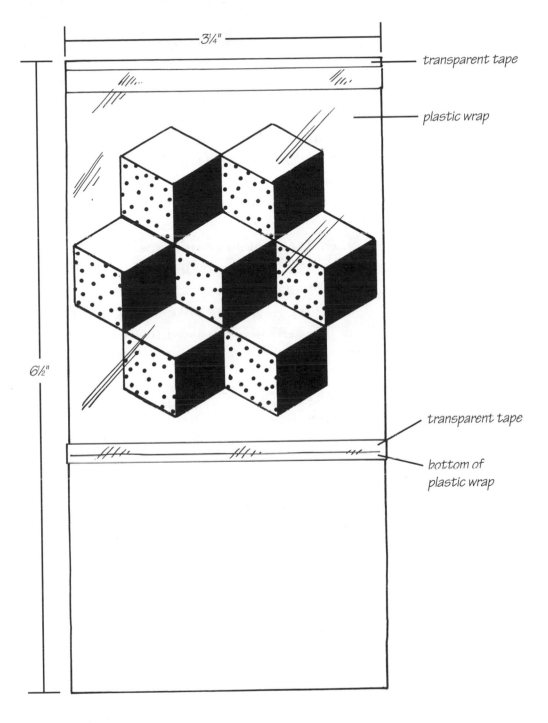

transparent tape

plastic wrap

transparent tape

bottom of plastic wrap

3¼"

6½"

PROJECT SPICED ACORN SQUASH

Squash was one of the many foods that the first European settlers learned about from the Native Americans who befriended them. The different varieties of squash were valued additions to the food supply because they were easy to grow and they could be stored for several months. By the time of the American Revolution, Americans had devised dozens of different recipes for each type of squash. The recipe you'll follow is based on the original Indian way of cooking acorn squash with maple syrup—another Native American contribution. It is particularly tasty with any roast meat or poultry.

INGREDIENTS

2 medium-size acorn squash
4 tablespoons butter (½ stick)
¼ cup brown sugar
½ teaspoon cinnamon
¼ teaspoon grated nutmeg
¼ teaspoon ground cloves
¼ teaspoon salt
4 tablespoons maple syrup
1 to 2 cups boiling water

EQUIPMENT

large serrated knife
cutting board
teaspoon
baking dish with sides 1½ to 2 inches high
small saucepan
teakettle
small mixing bowl
mixing spoon
paring knife
adult helper

MAKES

4 servings

1. Preheat the oven to 350 degrees F.

2. Place the squash on a cutting board and ask your adult helper to cut them in half. Use a teaspoon to scrape out the seeds and fibers. Place the four halves in the baking dish with the cut sides facing up, and set the dish aside.

3. Put the butter in the saucepan and heat it over low heat until it's melted.

4. Fill the teakettle part way with tap water and heat it to boiling. (You'll need 1 to 2 cups of boiling water.)

5. While the water is heating, measure the sugar, cinnamon, nutmeg, cloves, and salt into the mixing bowl. Use a mixing spoon to stir in the melted butter. Stir well to blend all the ingredients.

6. Pour an equal amount of the spice mixture into the hollow of each squash half. Add 1 tablespoon of maple syrup to each.

7. Ask your adult helper to pour boiling water into the baking dish to a depth of about 1 inch.

8. Place the baking dish in the middle of the oven. Bake for about an hour. The squash is done when you can easily poke the tip of a paring knife into it. Serve hot.

Camp Followers

Most officers in the Continental Army and the militia were served meals by regimental cooks and other staff, but the common soldiers were on their own. Some worked with friends to share cooking and cleanup duties. But roughly half the men could rely on their wives or girlfriends who traveled with the armies. The women, called camp followers, not only prepared meals, but also washed and mended clothes, took care of the sick and wounded, and occasionally found themselves in the thick of the fighting. The armies usually provided basic food supplies and the camp followers were alloted their share. Even the British and Hessians often had their wives and children nearby, having brought them from Europe.

MR. FRANKLIN PAYS A VISIT

When Peggy's father announced that Benjamin Franklin was coming for tea, everyone in the Wentworth household was excited, including the lodgers and the servants. Franklin had known Alexander Wentworth since the 1750s, when they had worked together recruiting militia for the French and Indian War. As an author, printer, inventor, scientist, and delegate to the Congress, Franklin was the most famous person in America. He was preparing to sail to France to try to persuade the French government to become America's ally in the war against Great Britain.

Franklin was aware that Peggy's parents opposed the Patriot cause, but he said nothing about it and they hardly talked about the war during his visit. Instead, he told amusing stories, shook hands with each of the lodgers, and was very kind to Peggy. He even helped her fix a problem with a hand puppet she was making. During afternoon tea, he asked Peggy to help him with a tray of wineglasses and a pitcher of water. They used these to entertain the gathering by

playing tunes on one of Mr. Franklin's inventions—the glass harmonica.

PROJECT BEN FRANKLIN'S GLASS HARMONICA

Benjamin Franklin experimented with something that most people have observed—that tapping partly filled glasses produces different musical-sounding notes. By placing several glasses in a row, each with less water than the glass to the left, he produced the glass harmonica. In 1761, he took the idea further by arranging a series of glass bowls suspended on a rod inside a box that looked like a small upright piano. As the rod was turned by a foot pedal, the rims of the bowls were moistened in a tray of water, and the player rubbed or tapped the moist rims to produce different notes. Franklin called his instrument an "armonica" and it quickly became popular throughout America and Europe. Composers, including Wolfgang Amadeus Mozart and Ludwig van Beethoven, wrote music for it.

Since most families could not afford an armonica, they learned to make music with Franklin's simpler glass harmonica—the same instrument you'll make in this activity. With patience and some practice, you'll be able to produce lovely notes and then entire tunes.

MATERIALS
large tray or countertop
8 identical glasses, as tall and thin as possible
large pitcher of water
towel or sponge
2 pencils, stir sticks, or chopsticks

1. Arrange the glasses in a row on the tray or countertop. Tall, thin glasses, like those used for wine or champagne, work best. *Note:* Make sure you have permission to use your family's best glassware. All the glasses must be the same and made of glass, not plastic.

2. Place the pitcher of water near the glasses and have a sponge or towel handy for spills.

3. With eight glasses, you can produce the eight-note scale: do, re, mi, fa, so, la, ti, do. Begin by filling the glass on the far left about ¾ full with water. Moisten your finger and rub it on the rim of the glass to produce a note. If you have trouble making this work, try moistening the rim of the glass and tapping it gently with a stir stick, pencil, or chopstick. When you're pleased with the low sound of do, go on to the next glass.

4. Put a little less water in the second glass. Continue from left to right, with a little less water for each glass. The last glass should have very little water.

The Amazing Mr. Franklin

People in the 1700s admired anyone who could do many different things and do them well. This is one reason Benjamin Franklin was so widely admired. Few individuals in any age have been so successful in so many different ways. While he was becoming wealthy as a printer, he also devoted some of his energy to improving life, especially in his beloved city of Philadelphia. His leadership made it the first city to have such improvements as street lighting, a fire department, a hospital, a lending library, and a paid police force. His Franklin stove remained the best home-heating system for a century, and his work with electricity made him one of the world's leading scientists. Perhaps most important, he played an important part in shaping America's democracy and in winning independence.

5. When all of the glasses are ready, start testing up and down the eight-note scale. When you find a glass that doesn't sound right, try changing the water level.

6. Keep practicing and experimenting until you have the scale, and then try your hand at producing tunes. Some people have the best results by rubbing their moistened finger on the rim; others have more success tapping the notes. Use whichever method works best for you and, in time, you'll be able to play with two fingers or two tappers.

PROJECT PAPIER-MÂCHÉ HAND PUPPETS

Hand puppets first became popular in Europe in the 1600s, and settlers brought this entertainment form to America. Puppeteers performed their plays on street corners or village greens, partly because many towns outlawed theaters as being against God's law. In the years leading up to, and during, the Revolution, Patriots used hand puppets to poke fun at King George III and his officials.

The directions here are for making a single hand puppet out of papier-mâché. If you haven't worked with this material before, you'll quickly find that it's like making your own modeling clay. (Papier-mâché is a French term meaning "mashed paper.") If you work with a friend, you can make two or more hand puppets and create your own play about Revolutionary War days. The puppet described here makes a good Ben Franklin, for example, and you could make one with a crown and a red or purple robe to represent France's King Louis XVI or Great Britain's King George III. Use library books to find out about Franklin's adventures in both of those royal courts.

Note: You should count on about seven days for the papier-mâché to dry before you can paint it.

MATERIALS

empty 1-liter plastic bottle with screw-on cap
scrap of thin cardboard or poster board, about 4 inches square
ruler
scissors
transparent tape
paper towels
several sheets of newspaper
pencil
white glue
teakettle
medium mixing bowl
mixing spoon
measuring cup
¼ cup all-purpose flour
small saucepan
large clean juice can or coffee can
oil of cloves or wintergreen (optional)
colander
piece of sandpaper
acrylic paints
small brush
¼ yard brown felt
stapler
scraps of gray or brown yarn (for hair)
2 pipe cleaners
adult helper

1. Fill the plastic bottle with water and screw the cap on tightly. The bottle will be a stand for working on the puppet and can also be used for storing it.

2. Roll the square piece of thin cardboard or poster board into a tube shape that fits snugly over the top of the bottle. Use transparent tape to hold the tube together.

3. To make a foundation for the puppet's head, wad two or three paper towels into a ball shape— as tight as you can make it. Use several pieces of tape to hold the ball together.

4. Spread several sheets of newspaper over your work surface, then use the tip of a pencil to make a hole in the paper-towel ball. Pour enough white glue into the hole to fill it. Let it soak in a minute, and then work the cardboard tube into it. Leave about 1 inch of cardboard sticking out below the ball. Place the foundation and tube over the top of the bottle to dry.

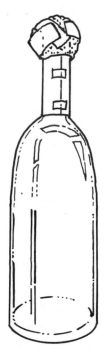

5. Pour 2 or 3 cups of water into a teakettle and ask your adult helper to bring it to a boil. While the water is heating, tear paper towels or newspapers into tiny pieces, making enough to fill the mixing bowl halfway (packed fairly tightly). Tearing is better than cutting because the jagged edges have more sticking power.

6. Have the adult pour enough boiling water into the bowl to barely cover the paper. Stir with a mixing spoon and let the paper soak for 10 to 15 minutes while you make the papier-mâché paste.

7. To make the paste, measure ¼ cup of flour into a saucepan and stir in about ¾ cup of water. Continue stirring until all lumps are gone. With the adult's help, cook the flour mixture over medium-high heat, stirring constantly, for about 3 minutes, or until it becomes a thick, smooth paste.

8. Ask your helper to pour the paste into the juice can to cool. If you think you'll have leftover paste that you'll want to save for another project, stir in a few drops of oil of cloves or oil of wintergreen to preserve it. Wash the saucepan before the paste hardens.

9. Pick up the soaked paper a handful at a time, squeeze out as much water as you can, and place the paper in the colander. Continue until all the paper is in the colander.

10. Return a handful or two of the paper to the mixing bowl. Pour some of the paste into the bowl and mix with your hands until it feels like moist clay. This is called papier-mâché pulp, or mash.

11. Spread some paste on the foundation for the head. This will help to hold the first layer of mash. Now use the mash as if it were clay, applying it in layers, gradually building the head to the size you want and forming features like a nose and ears.

Hint: Hand puppets were cartoonlike characters and their faces had to be recognizable from a distance. For this reason, their features were exaggerated so they would stand out; a character with a large nose, for example, was given a *very* large nose. It's also helpful to keep in mind that papier-mâché shrinks as it dries.

12. When you're satisfied with how your puppet looks, store it on its stand in a warm place for 7 days.

13. When the papier-mâché is dry, you can smooth over rough spots with a piece of sandpaper. Don't overdo the sanding; hand puppets traditionally had a rough look.

14. Keep the puppet's head on the stand for painting. Paint all the papier-mâché surfaces—this will help preserve it. You can either paint on some hair or glue on scraps of gray or brown yarn. Paint the eyes white and add blue or brown pupils after the white has dried (10 to 15 minutes).

15. To add spectacles, bend pipe cleaners into the shape of glasses and attach them with a little glue.

16. Clothing should be very simple. Even a piece of felt wrapped around your hand can be enough. For a slightly more elaborate outfit—a brown suit—copy the pattern shown here by drawing it with pencil on a piece of brown felt. Use the measurements shown but, for the width, measure it against your hand to make sure it will be a comfortable fit. (Allow about ½ inch on each side for the seam.) Cut out two identical pieces.

17. With the right sides facing in, staple the two pieces together. Place the staples close together for a firm seam, but be sure to leave openings at the top, the bottom, and the end of each arm. Turn the garment right side out, fit it around the cardboard tube neck, and glue it to the cardboard. Let the glue dry for 10 to 15 minutes.

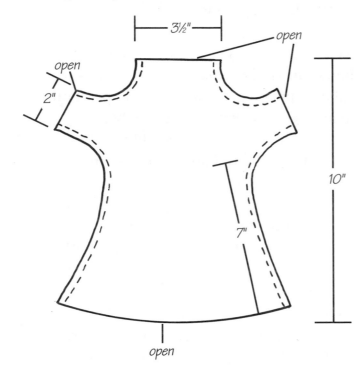

18. You're now ready for your hand puppet's audition. Carefully lift the puppet off the stand and fit it over your hand, with index finger in the head and thumb and middle finger in the arms.

Practice different movements with the head and arms. You'll quickly see that your puppet can do all sorts of things, like bowing, showing surprise, even bending over to pick something up.

19. With another puppet or two, you can create your own play about the American Revolution. For a stage, simply tape a sheet across a doorway and stand or sit behind it so that only the puppets are visible.

SCHOOL DAYS FOR PEGGY

Peggy was thrilled when she received a lovely handwritten notice that Miss Carter's Academy for Young Ladies was about to reopen. While she could walk to the school, many of the girls were boarders whom Peggy had not seen for several months. The school was famous throughout America because it offered the girls academic subjects like reading, arithmetic, and grammar, as well as more traditional lessons in music, drawing, painting, and needlework. Families from as far away as New York and Williamsburg, Virginia, sent their daughters to Miss Carter's.

The first project in the painting class was to make a small watercolor landscape by copying a picture that hung on the classroom wall. Peggy was pleased with how her little painting came out, so she decided to make a cloth-covered frame for it. In needlework instruction, she made two embroidered pockets for her mother, one to hold sewing items, the other for household things like keys and coins. Since lessons were given in the morning, Peggy sometimes had an afternoon to spend with her friend Anne from Baltimore. They often played games, such as marbles

or hoop rolling. They also made tops to see who could make one that would spin the longest.

PROJECT TOPS

Children in the 1700s had few toys or games—
and very little time to play with either. They
knew that it was more important for them to
contribute to the family's well-being and to learn
the skills they would need as adults, including
the complicated skills of managing a household,
preserving and preparing food, making and
mending clothing. Young people also had a lively
sense of fun; they combined work with play
whenever possible and, when they did have time,
they made the most of whatever games or toys
they could create themselves or with the help of
an adult. Tops were easy to make, for example,
requiring very little material or time. The chal-
lenge was to make a top that would spin longer
than any made by friends. Try this with a friend
or two and see who can make the longest-
spinning top.

MATERIALS
piece of thin cardboard, about 4 inches square
pencil
drawing compass, or a glass about 3½ inches in
*   diameter*
scissors
felt-tip pens or crayons, any colors
lollipop stick, or cotton swab with the cotton
*   scraped off*
penknife (to be used by an adult)
white glue
adult helper

1. Place the piece of cardboard on your work surface and use a glass or a compass to draw a circle
about 3½ inches in diameter. If you use a glass,
you'll have to figure out where the exact center of
your circle is. You can find this by first measuring
the diameter of the circle (the longest distance
across the circle). Let's say it's 3⅝ inches. Measure
another 3⅝ inch line across the circle; where the
two lines meet is the center. Push a pencil point,
or the compass tip, through the cardboard exactly
at the center point.

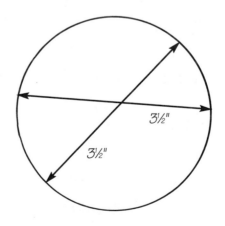

2. Carefully cut out the circle and draw a design on it. You can use either of the patterns shown here or create your own.

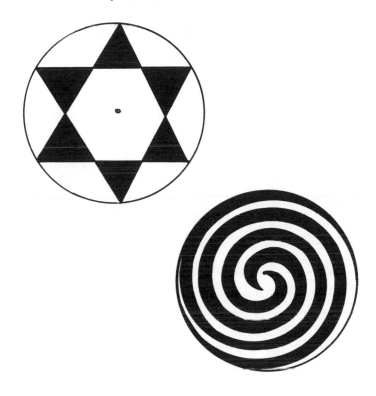

3. Use felt-tip pens or crayons to color your design.

4. Ask your adult helper to use a penknife to taper one end of a lollipop stick or cotton swab stick. The tip should be slightly rounded rather than a sharp point.

5. Work the stick through the hole in your cardboard circle, with the design on top. Only ¼ to ½ inch of the stick should be below the circle and the stick should be perfectly vertical (straight up and down).

6. Put a few drops of glue around the stick where it goes through the hole. Let the glue dry for 10 to 15 minutes.

7. Spin the top by holding it against a flat surface, as shown, and watch the pattern of colors change as it spins. *Note:* Be careful not to spin the top on any surface that could be damaged by the pointed tip. Try making more tops to see if you can lengthen the spinning time. You can try different materials or diameters for the circle and, for the stick, substitute a large pin, a nail, or a pencil.

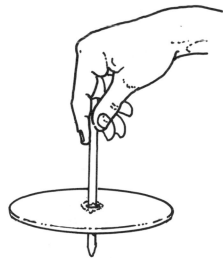

PROJECT FABRIC-COVERED PICTURE FRAME

After 1750, most American families could afford a few more luxuries than their parents or grandparents had enjoyed. One sign of this greater wealth was the increased use of fabrics to decorate their homes. People now used more cloth for curtains, wall hangings, and floor coverings. In addition, fabrics were used to cover chair seats, books, and frames for mirrors or pictures. In this project, you'll make a decoration for your room—or a special gift—by constructing a picture frame and covering it with fabric. Calico makes an attractive cover, or you may prefer a solid color. You can even mix fabrics by covering the back with a solid color and the front with a print.

MATERIALS
several sheets of newspaper
2 pieces of stiff cardboard, 7 inches square, and
  1 piece 3 by 4 inches
ruler
pencil
scissors
craft knife
old magazine or cutting board
3 pieces of fabric: 2 pieces 8 inches square; 1 piece
  3 by 4 inches
fabric glue, craft glue, or white glue

cloth mending tape in color to match fabric, or clear
  packaging tape
photograph, 4 inches square
adult helper

1. Spread the newspaper on your work surface.

2. With ruler and pencil, draw an outline for the picture opening in the middle of one 7-inch cardboard square. As shown in the diagram, the opening will be 4 inches square and each side will be 1½ inches from the outside edge.

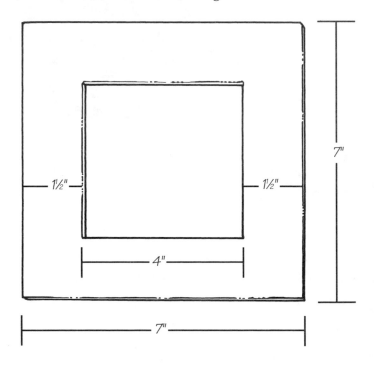

3. Place the marked cardboard on an old magazine or a cutting board. Have your adult helper use the craft knife to cut out the 4-by-4-inch opening. This will be the front of the frame.

4. Place one 8-inch fabric square on your work surface with the right side facing down. Center the uncut cardboard square on it so that ½ inch of fabric shows on each of the four sides. Cut off the 4 fabric corners with scissors, as shown.

5. Spread a layer of glue all the way around the edge of the cardboard, but not more than ½ inch in from the edge. Fold each of the cloth flaps over and press it against the cardboard.

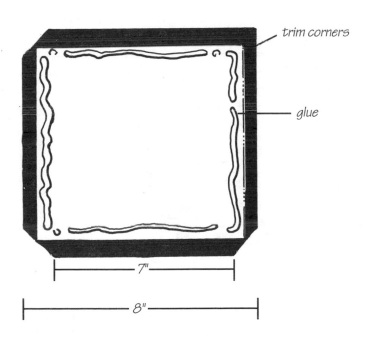

trim corners

glue

7"

8"

6. Place the other fabric square on your work surface, right side down, and position the front cardboard on it, with ½ inch of fabric visible on all sides. With a pencil, draw a line at each of the corners where you'll trim the fabric, and draw an X from corner to corner of the opening, as shown.

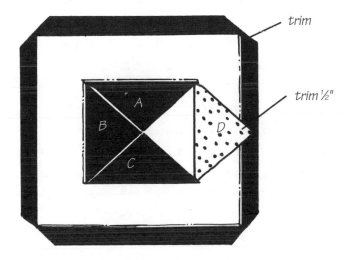

trim

trim ½"

A

B

C

D

7. Remove the cardboard. Use scissors to trim the four corners and to cut straight along the X lines to create four flaps, or ask your adult helper to cut the fabric X with the craft knife.

8. Position the cardboard on the wrong side of the fabric again. Fold each of the center flaps from the opening onto the cardboard, as shown in the drawing by flap D. Trim about ½ inch off the tip of each flap, spread glue on the cardboard underneath, and press the flap in place.

9. Fold the outside pieces of fabric over the card-board and glue them in place.

10. To attach the front of the frame to the back, place the front of the frame facedown on your work surface. Spread glue on either side of the picture opening and below it. But don't glue the space above the opening—you'll need that for inserting the picture.

11. Use the 3-by-4-inch cardboard to make a support, or stand, for the frame. First, cut the cardboard so that it measures 2 inches wide at the top and 3 inches wide at the bottom, as shown in the diagram.

12. Cut a piece of fabric to fit one side of the stand and glue it in place. Attach the stand to the middle of the frame with tape, as shown. Your frame is now ready. Slide a 4-by-4-inch photo-graph in the opening from the top and adjust the stand.

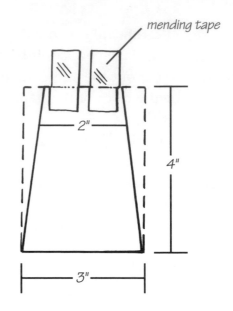

mending tape

2"

4"

3"

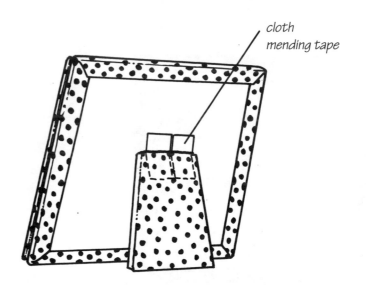

cloth
mending tape

PROJECT CREWEL EMBROIDERY POCKET

In the 1700s, women's skirts, which were called "petticoats," did not have pockets. Instead, a woman reached through a slit in the side of her petticoat to reach her "pocket"—a cloth bag tied around her waist in which she kept sewing items, coins, keys, and other personal belongings. Pockets were also hung on the backs of chairs or on a hook. These "wall pockets" kept small objects out of sight but within easy reach.

Like almost everything made of cloth, pockets were decorated with colorful designs, usually in a form of embroidery called crewelwork. (The word *crewel* refers to the two-ply wool yarn used.) You'll find that crewelwork is quite easy, almost like drawing with stitches, and the wool yarn covers an area quickly. You can use your finished pocket as a wall hanging, or hang it from a hook or chair back and use it for storing personal items. All of the supplies you'll need are inexpensive and can be purchased wherever sewing or embroidery materials are sold.

MATERIALS

2 pieces of white cotton or linen fabric, each about 10 inches long and 8 inches wide

ruler

pencil

scissors

scrap paper

small embroidery hoop, 4 to 6 inches in diameter (optional)

2-ply wool embroidery yarn—any 3 or 4 colors

crewel needle

about 24 straight pins

about 3 yards of bias tape, ⅞ inch to 1 inch wide, in color to match your yarns

sewing needle

thread in color to match tape

Behind the Art of Needlework

People admire early American needlework for the artistry of the design, colors, and stitching. Let's imagine what might be involved for a teenage girl creating such an item in the 1700s.

Unless she was the daughter of wealthy parents, she probably helped grow the flax and raise the sheep. She then took part in the soaking and pounding of the flax to produce linen fibers and, while the men probably sheared the sheep, she would have scoured and carded the fleece. She then spun linen fibers into thread on a small wheel, or walked beside the large spinning wheel to spin the wool fibers into yarn. The thread or yarn could then be woven into cloth, or she might decide to use it for needlework. In either case, she often had the messy task of dyeing, using a pot of natural dyes made from leaves, berries, bark, or other material she had gathered. After these many hours of labor, she would finally be ready to practice her skills in needlework.

1. Spread the fabric on your work surface. Use ruler and pencil to copy the outline for the pocket directly onto the fabric. The piece should measure about 4 inches wide at the top and slant to about 8 inches at the widest point. The bottom is rounded, as shown.

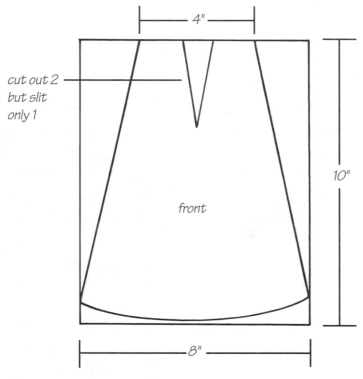

cut out 2
but slit
only 1

4"

10"

front

8"

2. Cut out the fabric piece with scissors and use it as a template to make a second piece exactly the same. Measure and cut a slit, about 3½ inches long, in just one piece, as shown. This will be the front of the pocket and also the piece that you embroider.

3. You can either use the folk art design shown here or create your own. If you make your own design, sketch it first on a piece of scrap paper—and remember to keep it simple. Copy the final design on the right side of the front fabric piece.

4. The parts labeled green (but use any color you wish) can be embroidered with a running stitch. To make a running stitch, bring the needle up at A, go down at B, then up at C, down at D, and so on. If you feel more comfortable working with an embroidery hoop, center the design over the smaller hoop and press the larger hoop in place over it.

running stitch

5. For the portions labeled rose and blue, use a backstitch to make a more solid line. To back-stitch, bring the needle up at A, down at B, up at

C, then down at A again before coming up at D, and continue. If you find you're enjoying the needlework, you can try filling in the rose portions by placing stitches close together. You can even switch to different shades of the same color, making it darker toward the center.

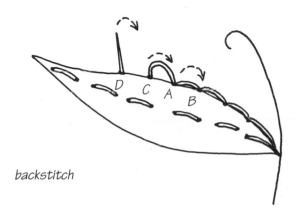

backstitch

6. Continue until you've embroidered the entire design.

7. Cut a piece of bias tape as long as the slit. Fold the tape over so that half of it is on the front of the slit, half on the back side. Thread a sewing needle with thread that matches the tape color and sew the tape onto the right-hand side of the slit.

8. Repeat step 7 for the left-hand side of the slit.

9. Now place the front and back of the pocket together, with the right sides facing out. Pin the two pieces together with straight pins.

10. Beginning at the right side, fold the tape so that half is on the front and half on the back. As you sew, you'll be closing the seam. You can cut the tape in shorter lengths to make it more convenient to work with. Sew about ¼ inch in from the edge, using a running stitch. Make sure your needle goes through both layers of tape and both layers of the pocket.

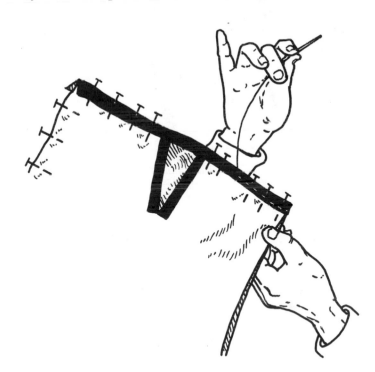

11. Continue attaching the tape all the way around. Sew completely across the top of the pocket so that the only way into the pocket is through the slit.

12. Cut two lengths of tape, each about 18 inches long. Sew one on either side of the pocket at the top, as shown. Tie the ends together in a bow or a square knot and hang your finished pocket on a chair back or hook, with your crewelwork showing for everyone to enjoy.

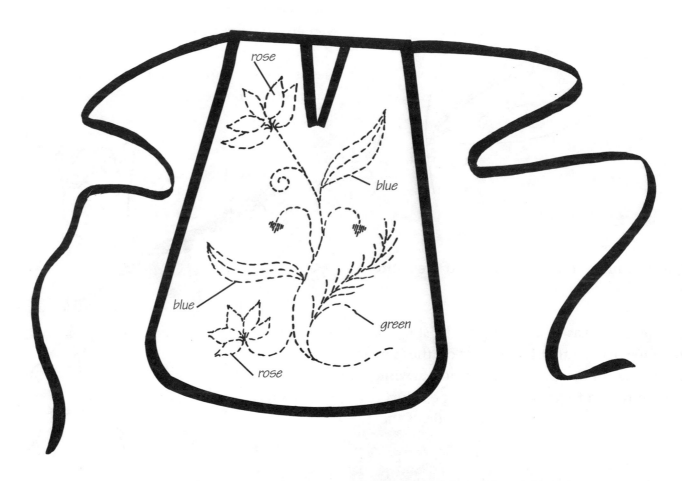

CHAPTER FOUR

WINTER

From the parlor window, Peggy watched people rushing along Philadelphia's snowy streets. Confusion and fear had gripped the city for three days, ever since the news arrived that Washington's Continental Army had crossed the Delaware River into Pennsylvania. Peggy was amazed that instead of being cheered by the news, people saw it as a sign of defeat. Many Patriots were packing to leave. Peggy's father predicted that General Washington would soon have to surrender and the British would march into Philadelphia.

No one yet knew that Washington was not at all ready to surrender. In spite of the defeats and the bitter cold of an early winter, the ragged soldiers were still ready to fight for independence. Even they did not know that Washington was already planning a way to strike back.

SAYING GOOD-BYE

During the first weeks of December, Peggy and her family watched horse-drawn carriages and ox-drawn wagons leaving the city. Many of their Patriot friends were heading for farm villages where they could stay with relatives or friends. Others followed the Continental Congress to Baltimore.

The crisis in America's Revolution led both of Peggy's brothers to make decisions. Robert, who was nineteen, announced that he would join a Loyalist regiment when the British came to Philadelphia. Thomas, two years younger, said he would leave the city with the carpenter he worked for as an apprentice. Silas Greene, the carpenter, and his wife, Abigail, were staunch Patriots and Peggy's parents guessed that the Greenes and Thomas would end up in Washington's encampment. Tom would only say he was not sure what he would do but that he would write soon.

In the few days before he left, Tom spent long hours discussing the war and his plans with

his father. He also spent time with Peggy. He showed her how to make a pair of moccasins like the ones frontiersmen and Indians wore, and he helped her finish work on a planter for the windowsill in her room.

ᴘʀᴏᴊᴇᴄᴛ **PEGGED-PINE PLANTER**

In the 1770s, most Americans still made many of their own household furnishings, although special pieces would be turned over to a carpenter, or joiner. Nails were expensive, so entire pieces were often"joined" without a single nail. Wooden pegs, sometimes called tree nails, were one common substitute. Although you will be using nails in this project, you'll still get a good idea of what it was like to work with pegs.

Early Americans often painted their furniture, but when an extra-fine finish was desired, they hand-rubbed it with concoctions like linseed oil mixed with cider. With a few modern shortcuts, you'll obtain a smooth, glossy finish, and you'll feel the excitement of giving new life to raw wood. Your planter is intended for indoor use only and plants should first be placed in a container, such as an aluminum foil baking pan or a yogurt container.

Note: Take your measurements to the lumber-supply store and ask for clear pine shelving (that is, without knots); they may give you scrap pieces for very little. You should also know that wood is sold in a 1-inch thickness, but this is a "carpenter's measure," which will actually be ¾ inch thick, and a board 6 inches wide will probably be 5¾ inches.

MATERIALS

piece of thin paper (or tracing paper)

pencil

scissors

2 pieces of 1-inch pine shelving: 1 piece 6 by 11 inches; 1 piece 4 by 36 inches

T square or carpenter's level (optional)

workbench with vise, or 2 "C" clamps

coping saw

hand saw (finishing saw—with many short teeth close together)

¾-inch and ¼-inch drill bits, hand drill, or electric drill

about 24 1-inch finishing nails

nail set (or 1 large nail)

hammer

¼-inch wood dowel, about 6 inches long

several sheets of newspaper

white glue, or carpenter's glue

2 sheets of sandpaper—medium grit and very fine grit

4 or 5 clean rags

small can of wood stain—pine, "Colonial," or any other light shade

paste wax

small aluminum foil baking pan or sturdy yogurt container

adult helper

1. With pencil and thin paper, make the pattern for the back piece of the planter. Also draw an X to mark the center of the hole. Cut out the pattern and position it on the 6-inch piece of wood. Trace around the pattern with pencil.

3. While the back piece is still clamped, use a hand drill or have your adult helper use the electric drill to drill a ¾-inch hole, as shown. Position the tip of the drill on the penciled X.

4. With the adult's help, use the finishing saw to cut the other four pieces from the 4-inch-wide board: 1 bottom piece 9½ inches long; 1 front piece 11 inches long; and 2 end pieces each 4 inches long. You can use a T square or a carpenter's level to make sure your corners are square.

5. Nail one 4-by-4-inch end piece to each end of the 9½-inch bottom piece, as shown in the drawing.

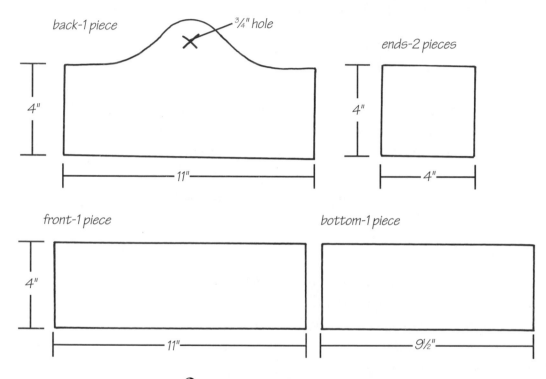

back-1 piece ¾" hole

X

ends-2 pieces

4"

11"

4"

4"

front-1 piece

bottom-1 piece

4"

11"

9½"

2. Place the piece of wood in a vise, or clamp it with "C" clamps, and ask your adult helper to use the coping saw to cut the curved lines. Straight lines can be cut much more easily with a finishing saw.

Hint: Work slowly with the coping saw and let the saw do the work.

6. Lay the planter flat and position the back piece on it. Make sure all your corners line up and hammer about 6 nails along the bottom and 2 along the sides. (If the hammering is very hard, ask your adult helper to drill starter holes all the way through the back piece.)

7. Turn the planter over and attach the front piece the same way.

8. With the planter still front-side up, drill six holes in the front—three on either end as shown. Each hole should go all the way through the front piece and about ¼ inch into the side piece.

9. Cut a dowel to fit each hole by pushing the dowel all the way into the hole and then making a pencil line on the dowel. Ask your adult helper to use the coping saw to cut each dowel, making each just a fraction longer than the hole; each peg should extend only about ⅛ inch above the surface.

10. Spread newspaper on your work surface and place the planter on it. Put a little glue on the sides of each peg (but not the end) and use the hammer to tap it into the hole.

11. Use medium grit sandpaper to sand all the edges. Be sure to sand with the grain of the wood or the sandpaper will leave scratches that are very hard to remove. Round off the edges as you sand. Sand the pegs until they're exactly level with the pine, and here, too, make sure you sand with the grain of the pine. Very little sanding is needed on the inside of the planter.

12. Sand all the surfaces a second time with very fine sandpaper. Wipe off all the sanding dust with a clean rag.

13. Use a small rag to apply two coats of wood stain. Follow the directions on the can for drying times. It will be less messy if you stain the bottom of the planter first, then the inside, and then the outside.

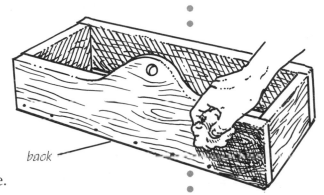

back

14. When the second coat of stain is dry, apply one or two coats of paste wax. Follow directions on the can for how to apply and how many coats to apply. As you buff the waxed sides, you'll see the soft, glossy finish emerge. Congratulations! Your pegged-pine planter is finished. Place it on a table or your desk. You can use your planter without a plant to hold pencils, pens, computer disk, or CDs. If you use it as a planter, remember to first line the planter with an aluminum foil baking tin or some other container.

front

MOCCASINS

The early European settlers in America learned how to make moccasins from the Native American peoples living along the Atlantic coast. This form of footwear remained popular throughout the 1700s because moccasins were comfortable, easy to make, and inexpensive. Pioneers on the western frontier continued to rely on them in the 1800s, and many people in the East continued to use them for indoor wear, like slippers.

You'll make your moccasins by following a simple one-piece design developed by the Algonquin tribes of eastern North America. While you can make moccasins out of leather, the stitching is much more difficult, so the directions here call for using chamois, either natural or artificial, available at most automotive departments or stores. Natural chamois is made from the hides of deer or other animals so it is close to the material used in the 1700s. Chamois is quite thin, however, so these moccasins are intended only for indoor use.

MATERIALS
large paper grocery bag
scissors
pencil
ruler
tape measure or piece of string
2 pieces of chamois (one chamois of the kind sold in automotive stores is large enough for one moccasin)
black felt-tip pen, fine point
large sewing needle
strong brown thread, or embroidery thread
2 rawhide thongs (sold as bootlaces; optional)

1. Open up the grocery bag, cut out one large panel, and place it on the floor.

2. Stand in the middle of the grocery-bag panel, barefoot or in socks. With pencil, trace around one of your feet.

3. In order to make a pattern like the one shown here, you first have to figure the width—the distance from A to B. To do this, wrap a tape measure or string around the widest part of your foot. With ruler and pencil, draw a line that length on the grocery bag across the widest part of the outline of your foot, as shown by the dotted line from A to B.

4. Use ruler and pencil to draw another line through the longest part of the foot outline, as indicated in the drawing. (As shown, be sure to add ½ inch at either end for sewing the seam.) Notice also that there is a small notch in the heel.

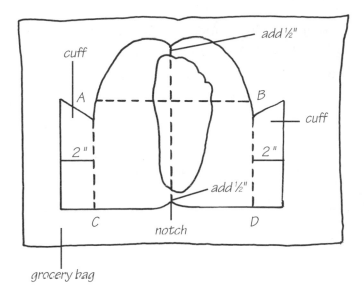

cuff

add ½"

A

B

cuff

2"

2"

add ½"

C

D

notch

grocery bag

5. Complete the pattern by drawing a straight line from A to C and B to D. Add the cuff lines and two rounded lines around the top.

6. Cut out the paper pattern and position it on one piece of chamois. Trace around the pattern with felt-tip pen and cut out the moccasin shape with scissors.

7. Repeat step 6 for the other moccasin (right and left are the same in this style).

8. Fold the chamois for one moccasin exactly in half. If your chamois has a right and wrong side, as fabric does, the right side should be on the inside. You'll sew one seam up the back and another from the toe to the start of the cuff, as shown.

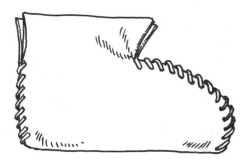

9. Sew the seams with a whipstitch, placing the stitches about ¼ inch apart. To whipstitch, place the two edges together and sew each stitch at an angle, going over the edge each time and pushing the needle through both layers, as shown in the drawing.

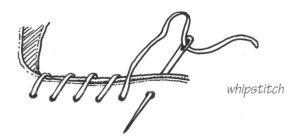

whipstitch

Moccasin Lore

Most Native American tribes and nations throughout North America used some form of moccasin, but there were important differences from tribe to tribe. A person's tribe could be identified by the style of moccasin he wore and often even by the footprint left by that moccasin. In time of war, some warriors might wear the moccasin of another tribe in order to trick an enemy. Most Iroquois frowned on this, because wearing the moccasin of a tribe indicated that you accepted the laws and customs of that tribe.

Moccasins were usually decorated with beads, paint, or colored porcupine quills, because Indians believed that footwear should be as beautiful as the ground one was walking on. In winter or rainy weather, many Indians wore an over-moccasin to protect the design. Special winter moccasins were also common, either stuffed with fur or with the fur left on the hide and worn on the inside.

10. When you've finished sewing the heel and the toe, turn the moccasin right side out and try it on.

11. Repeat steps 8 through 10 for the other moccasin. You can wear the cuffs up or fold them over, as shown. And, if you want a tighter fit, you can wrap a rawhide lace around each moccasin just underneath the cuff, as indicated in the drawing, and tie it in front.

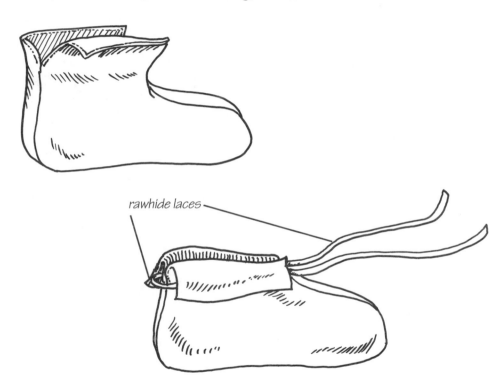

rawhide laces

CHRISTMAS AND WASHINGTON'S SURPRISE

The Christmas season of 1776 felt strange to Peggy and her family. Both the city and the Wentworths' lodging house seemed deserted with so many Patriots away, and it was unusually quiet with Thomas gone. Peggy was determined to be cheerful, however, and she made special holiday treats, like chewy noels, to serve the guests, and colorful packets of powdered cocoa for her friends.

Christmas itself was quiet, but the days that followed were packed with excitement. First came the amazing news that on Christmas night, General Washington had led his half-frozen Continental soldiers across the Delaware River and surprised the Hessian garrison at Trenton, New Jersey. The Patriots won a stunning victory, capturing hundreds of enemy soldiers and tons of supplies, while suffering only two men wounded. Washington then led his army on to Princeton, where they won another victory, this time over a British army. Suddenly the war looked entirely different, giving Americans renewed

hope that they could win their independence. As happy Patriot families streamed back into Philadelphia, one of the lodgers asked if Mrs. Wentworth would prepare a special meal to celebrate and she politely agreed. He gave her the recipe for a dish he said had been created by General Washington's cook.

PROJECT PHILADELPHIA PEPPER POT

Beginning in the winter of 1776–1777, the soldiers of the Continental Army suffered through three straight winters of near-starvation and bone-chilling cold. One day, according to legend, General Washington asked his cook, Christopher Ludwick, if he could make any kind of meal that would boost the men's morale. Ludwick had little to work with that day—potatoes, some tripe, odds and ends, and spices, including lots of peppercorns. The cook combined everything he had into a thick soup or stew, which he named "Philadelphia Pepper Pot" in honor of his home city. The hot, spicy meal was perfect. It warmed the men, filled their stomachs, and gave their spirits a lift. Over the next few years, it became known as "the soup that won the war." Modern recipes, like the one you'll follow, offer a milder version of Philadelphia Pepper Pot.

INGREDIENTS

2 medium onions
2 celery sticks
½ green pepper
2 carrots
3 medium potatoes
3 tablespoons butter
1 pound lean ground beef
2 tablespoons flour
4 cups beef broth
2 cups water
2 teaspoons dried parsley
1 teaspoon salt
½ teaspoon crushed red pepper
½ teaspoon thyme
½ teaspoon black pepper, freshly ground, if possible

EQUIPMENT

large kettle or pot, with cover
large spoon
paring knife
cutting board
vegetable chopper
adult helper

MAKES

about 6 servings as main dish

1. Peel the onion and wash the celery, green pepper, carrots, and potatoes.

2. With an adult's help, use a paring knife or vegetable chopper to chop the onions, celery, green pepper, and carrots into little pieces. Cut or chop the potatoes into slightly larger pieces—about ½-inch cubes.

3. Melt the butter in the kettle.

4. Add the ground beef and cook until browned, stirring frequently to break it up.

5. Add the celery, green peppers, carrots, and potatoes. Cook slowly over low heat for 10 to 12 minutes. Add a little water if the mixture becomes dry or sticks to the kettle.

6. Stir in the flour and cook for about 5 minutes more, stirring often.

7. Add the beef broth, water, dried parsley, salt, red pepper, thyme, and black pepper. Stir well, then cover.

8. Bring the stew to a boil, then lower the heat and simmer for 15 minutes. Serve in large soup bowls as the main dish for supper. With whatever beverage you serve, raise your glasses in a toast to Chef Ludwick, General Washington, and America's independence!

Food in Revolutionary War Days

Continental soldiers and militiamen sometimes were short of food and poor people often suffered from malnutrition or scurvy because of poor diets. Except for these special situations, the American people enjoyed an amazing abundance and variety of foods. A visitor to New York's open-air market, for example, counted sixty-three different kinds of fish on sale, fourteen varieties of shellfish, fifty-two kinds of meat and fowl, and twenty-seven kinds of vegetables. Pigs and chickens roamed freely because they could forage for their food. A whole pig could be purchased for fifty cents. And people everywhere could walk into open country to fish; to hunt wild turkey, deer, and other game; or to gather grapes, berries, nuts, and other wild foods.

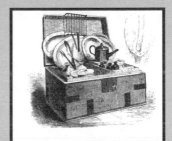

$\overline{PROJECT}$ CHEWY NOELS

The origin of this delicious recipe, and the name, are unknown, but these little snack or dessert squares have been a holiday tradition for more than two hundred years. You'll find that the recipe is easy to follow and takes surprisingly little time. If you enjoy chewy noels, you can make them any time of year.

INGREDIENTS

2 tablespoons butter
2 eggs
1 teaspoon vanilla
1 cup dark brown sugar
5 tablespoons all-purpose flour
⅛ teaspoon baking soda
¼ teaspoon salt
1 cup chopped walnuts or pecans
¼ cup confectioners' sugar

EQUIPMENT

9-inch-square baking pan
medium-size mixing bowl
eggbeater or whisk
large mixing spoon
wax paper
table knife
adult helper

MAKES
24 to 30 squares, about 6 servings

1. Preheat the oven to 350 degrees F.

2. Place the butter in the baking pan and melt it over low heat on the stove top or in the oven.

3. Break the eggs into the mixing bowl, add the vanilla, and beat lightly. (Always wash your hands after handling raw eggs.)

4. Stir the brown sugar, flour, baking soda, and salt into the eggs. Mix well with a mixing spoon or the eggbeater.

5. Stir in the chopped nuts.

6. Slowly pour the batter into the baking pan on top of the melted butter. *Don't* stir.

7. Bake for about 25 minutes until firm to the touch. Ask your adult helper to remove the pan from the oven, and turn the cake onto a sheet of wax paper to cool, butter side up.

8. Sprinkle powdered sugar on top, cut into squares, serve, and enjoy!

LOOKING AHEAD

In late January 1777, the Wentworths received a letter from Thomas, saying that he had joined the Continental Army and they were in winter quarters at Morristown, New Jersey. Although Peggy's parents were not happy with this news, she was surprised at how calmly they accepted it. Like many people with Loyalist sympathies, they still hoped that the war could be ended without America's becoming independent. No one could know in January 1777 that the fighting would last for another five years. Nor could anyone know that with France as an ally, the Americans would eventually win the war and, with it, their independence.

For her part, Peggy was thrilled by the recent victories and by the news that Tom was now a Continental soldier. To celebrate, she and Anne held a tea party in a private room of the lodging house with four other girls from their school. During the afternoon, the girls had fun playing games and making Pennsylvania Dutch valentines to give to friends. When Peggy placed the teapot on the herbal hotplate she had made in needlework class, she was delighted with the delicate aroma that spread through the room.

PROJECT · HERBAL HOTPLATE

Early Americans used dozens of herbs in their cooking and in home remedies for illness or injury. They also used them for decoration and as air fresheners. In this project, you'll make a hotplate filled with herbs; when you place a hot dish or pot on it, you'll release the pleasing fragrance of the herbs.

For your herbal hotplate, you can choose a single herb with a distinctive scent, such as lavender, sage, or bay leaf, or you may prefer a combination of two or three different herbs. To help you decide, you can experiment by testing the aroma of the dried herbs in your kitchen or even fresh herbs from a garden or market. Use the hotplate at home, or give one as a memorable gift.

MATERIALS
2 pieces of loose weave cotton fabric, 9 inches square—any pattern
ruler
pencil
scissors
12 to 15 straight pins
sewing needle
thread, in color to match fabric
1 to 1½ cups dried herbs—sage, lavender, bay leaf, rosemary, marjoram, or any combination
large embroidery needle or tapestry needle

wool embroidery thread, about 16 inches, in color to match fabric or contrast with it

1. Spread the 9-inch fabric squares on your work surface. With scissors, clip off the corners, as shown.

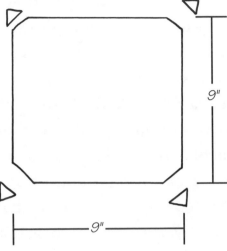

2. Place the two pieces together with right sides (or print sides) facing each other. With needle and matching thread, sew around the two squares, leaving a gap of about 2 inches in one side for filling. Sew a running stitch about ¼ inch in from the edge. To sew a running

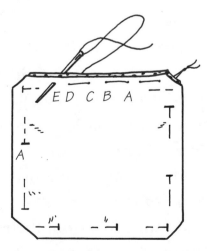

stitch, bring the needle up at A, go down at B, up again at C, down at D, and so on, as shown in the drawing.

3. When you've finished sewing the two pieces together, except for the 2-inch gap, tie a double knot at the end of the last stitch and cut off any extra thread.

4. Turn the fabric pieces right side out. Stuff the dried herbs through the gap.

5. Close the gap with a whipstitch. To whipstitch, bring the needle up through the fabric, stitch over the edges of the fabric at an angle and up again next to the previous stitch. See the drawing for whipstitching with the moccasin project.

6. The last step is called "tie quilting:" Cut a 12-inch piece of wool embroidery thread, and thread it through the eye of the large embroidery needle.

7. In one of the four locations (A, B, C, D), push the needle all the way through the layers of the hotplate from top to bottom, then back to the top again. Tie the thread tightly to indent the fabric like a quilt and cut off the extra thread.

8. Repeat step 7 at the other three locations, as shown. Your herbal hotplate is now ready for you to give as a gift or use in your own home.

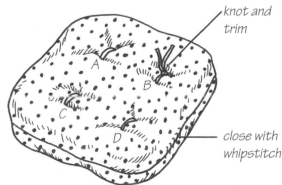

knot and trim

close with whipstitch

Herbal Aromas

In addition to using herbs for cooking and medicine, people found many different uses for the aroma of various herbs. Dried leaves of lavender and peppermint, for example, were sprinkled under rugs and along floorboards to freshen the air and to drive away mice. Basil leaves were used in the same way to repel ants and insects. On laundry days, "washing herbs" were added to the wash water to sweeten bed linens and discourage bugs.

Sachets—small bags of dried herbs—were placed in drawers and cupboards to keep clothes smelling fresh and to keep moths out. A special medicinal sachet made of marjoram, wood betony, rose petals and leaves, lavender, and cloves (a spice) was said to cure headaches, and many people wore one on a cord around the neck.

Another way to use the aroma of herbs was in a "decoction"—soaking the herb in water to extract the scent. People used a decoction of the herb feverfew to apply to their skin as a mosquito repellent. Another, made from pennyroyal, was said to rid dogs of fleas.

PROJECT ☆ A PATRIOT TEA PARTY

Afternoon tea was a custom that early settlers brought from England and it remained popular through the 1800s. In addition to providing a pause in the day's work, tea was a pleasant occasion for socializing, at least for those who could afford the time. Wealthier women frequently took their needlework when visiting a friend for tea.

In Revolutionary War days, however, American Patriots refused to drink tea because their conflict with Great Britain had involved a quarrel over tea, and tea was seen as a symbol of Britain's overbearing government. Patriot women served all sorts of substitutes, such as tea brewed from birch twigs and leaves, or from dried berry leaves. Herb teas, which are popular today, were another substitute. All of these beverages were called "liberty tea." And, instead of any kind of tea, some people turned to coffee or to mulled cider.

In this activity, you can try a liberty tea or mulled cider. Invite friends to a Patriot tea party with both berry tea and cider along with some cinnamon tea toasties. Look for berry teas that are sold loose leaf, rather than in bags, if possible, for a more authentic touch. In either case, brew the tea in a teapot instead of individual cups. Herbal and berry teas are now available at most supermarkets.

Liberty Tea

INGREDIENTS

about 12 teaspoons of berry leaves or wintergreen for 1 pot
6 cups boiling water
honey
lemon or milk to taste

EQUIPMENT

teakettle
teapot
small strainer
adult helper

MAKES

6 cups

1. Bring a kettle of water to a boil.

2. Place the tea leaves in the teapot and ask your adult helper to pour about 6 cups of boiling water into the pot. (Check the directions on the box for exactly how many teaspoons of tea to use for each cup.) Let the tea steep for about 5 minutes.

3. Place the strainer over each cup as you pour.

4. Serve liberty tea with honey and milk or lemon (not both, since the lemon would curdle the milk).

Mulled Cider

INGREDIENTS

4 cups apple cider
2 whole cloves
1 cinnamon stick
¼ teaspoon allspice
¼ cup light brown sugar

EQUIPMENT

medium-size saucepan
mixing spoon

MAKES

4 servings

1. Place the cider, cloves, cinnamon stick, and allspice in the saucepan. Heat over medium heat for about 5 minutes.

2. Stir in the brown sugar. Bring the cider to the boiling point, then lower the heat and simmer for another 5 minutes.

3. Remove the cloves and cinnamon stick with the mixing spoon and let the cider cool for a few minutes. Serve warm.

Cinnamon Tea Toasties

INGREDIENTS

½ cup sugar
2 teaspoons cinnamon
½ stick butter
small loaf of unsliced bread

EQUIPMENT

small bowl
teaspoon
small saucepan
bread knife
toast tongs or fork
shallow baking pan
serving plate
adult helper

MAKES

about 4 servings

1. Preheat the oven to 400 degrees F.

2. Measure the sugar and cinnamon into the small bowl. Stir with a teaspoon to mix thoroughly, then set aside.

3. Melt the butter in the saucepan.

4. With the adult's help, cut the bread into slices two inches thick. You'll need 3 or 4 slices, depending on the size of the loaf.

Boston Tea Party

When England's Parliament passed a Tea Act in 1773, American Patriots felt they had finally been pushed too far. The new law said that colonists would now have to buy all their tea from England's East India Company. To the Patriots, it looked as if England meant to control all their business affairs. When ships carrying the tea began arriving in American ports, angry Patriots locked up the tea or ordered the ships' captains to leave without unloading.

In Boston, a band of Patriots, disguised as Mohawk Indians, boarded three tea ships and dumped 342 casks of tea into Boston Harbor. Patriots everywhere cheered the news of the "Boston Tea Party," but the king and his officials passed a series of laws to punish the colonists and placed a military governor in charge at Boston. Within a year, the American Revolution had begun.

5. Cut off the crusts and cut each slice into thirds.

6. Remove the butter from the burner and let it cool a minute or two, but not harden.

7. Pick up a piece of the bread with tongs or a fork and dip it in the butter. Dip quickly, just enough to moisten the bread, rather than to soak up the butter. Place the bread in the baking pan and repeat with the other pieces. Sprinkle the cinnamon-sugar mixture over the top of all the pieces.

8. Bake for a few minutes, turning often, until all the pieces are evenly browned on both sides. Ask the adult to help you remove the pan from the oven. Place the toasties on a serving plate. Serve with hot tea or warm mulled cider.

PROJECT · PENNSYLVANIA DUTCH VALENTINE

Americans began to celebrate Valentine's Day in the 1740s. That was when they started the practice of making and giving valentines to special friends. These homemade cards remained popular until about 1870, when inexpensive, machine-printed cards began to replace them. The most elaborate handmade cards were produced by German settlers in Pennsylvania, people who were called "Pennsylvania Dutch" by other Americans. For your homemade valentine, you'll use a fairly simple design and a technique based on early Pennsylvania Dutch cards.

MATERIALS

sheet of white paper, 8½ by 11 inches
ruler
pencil
scissors
manicure scissors (optional)
8 to 10 straight pins, or removable transparent tape
old magazine
piece of corrugated cardboard, such as part of a cardboard carton
darning needle, or small nail
rubber cement, or substitute craft glue or white glue
1 sheet red construction paper, 8½ by 11 inches
fine-or medium-point black felt-tip pen or light-colored gel pen

1. On a sheet of white paper, use ruler and pencil to draw a 5-inch square. Cut out the square.

2. Fold the square in half. Copy the design shown here on the paper; notice how the design fits against the fold and where it touches the fold.

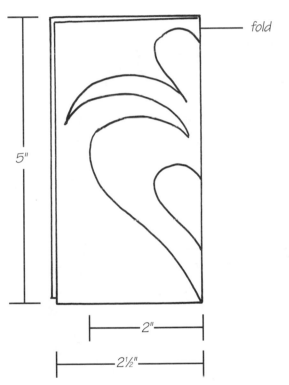

fold

5"

2"

2½"

3. Carefully cut out the design with scissors. For very tight curves, you might want to try manicure scissors.

4. Unfold the paper and flatten it. Place it on the piece of cardboard, with the magazine underneath. Fix it to the cardboard with straight pins or removable tape.

5. Make very light pencil marks around the design where you want to place pinholes. (The holes will show red on the finished valentine.) Space the pencil marks as evenly as you can.

darning needle or nail

cardboard

magazine

6. Use a darning needle or a nail to prick holes through each of the pencil marks.

7. Fold the red construction paper in half. Unpin the valentine design and center it on the construction paper. If the design looks too small, trim the construction paper. Or, if you prefer, use the construction paper unfolded as a single sheet and write your greeting above and below the white design, as shown. Use felt-tip pen or gel pen for the writing.

8. Spread a thin layer of rubber cement on the back of the white design. Turn it over, and press it in place on the construction paper. When the rubber cement is dry, you can rub off any excess cement. Your Pennsylvania Dutch valentine is now ready to give to a special person. To follow the traditions of the late 1700s, you should place the valentine on the person's doorstep, or have a messenger deliver it, rather than use the mail.

GLOSSARY

Algonquin Native American tribes living in eastern North America.

apprentice A person who is learning a skill or trade from someone who is skilled in that occupation.

armonica A musical instrument invented by Benjamin Franklin, which uses partially filled glass containers to produce musical notes.

buckskin Clothing made of soft animal hides, most commonly worn by Native Americans and frontier settlers.

camp follower A woman who followed her soldier husband during military campaigns and helped with cooking, washing, mending, and caring for the wounded or sick.

chamois Soft deer hide or other animal hide.

chapeaugraphy A parlor game of the 1700s that involved making hats in different shapes.

Continental Army The army, led by George Washington, that represented all thirteen states, making it the first national army.

Continental Congress   Beginning in April 1775, this Congress guided America through the Revolution, although it did not have many powers as a national government, such as the power to raise money through taxes.

crewel   Woolen thread used in some kinds of embroidery.

Declaration of Independence   The 1776 document in which the thirteen American states declared themselves free and independent of Great Britain.

decoction   Herbs soaked in water to release their aroma.

diorama   A three-dimensional scene or model, usually with a painted background.

Grand Union Flag   Approved by Congress in 1775, this was America's first national flag, although it still had the British Union Jack in the upper left corner.

Hessians   Mercenary soldiers from the states of Germany hired by King George III to help fight the Patriots in the American Revolution.

horn book   A paddle-shaped piece of wood holding a page of printing and covered with a thin, transparent piece of horn.

joiner   A carpenter or cabinetmaker in the 1700s.

Liberty Bell   The famous bell rung to signal the first public reading of the Declaration of Independence in Philadelphia and ever since a symbol of America's freedom and independence.

liberty tea   Tea made from herbs or berries as a substitute for regular tea and the beverage chosen by Patriots during the Revolutionary War era.

Loyalists   Americans who remained loyal to England during the Revolution, some of whom fought for the British.

mercenaries   Soldiers hired to fight for pay by a foreign country or ruler.

militia   Citizen soldiers who are trained to fight for their town or state.

Mohawk   One of the six tribes of the Iroquois nation in New York State.

musket   A long-barreled, single-shot gun that was the primary weapon of soldiers on both sides of the American Revolution.

Parliament   The law-making body, or legislature, of England.

Patriots   Americans who insisted on protecting their rights against England and who fought in, or supported, the Revolution.

petticoat A woman's dress in the 1700s.

pocket A separate pouch used by women to carry or store small personal items.

receipts The early American word for recipes.

redcoats Soldiers in the British army who wore bright red, or scarlet, coats.

rifle A long-barreled gun used by expert marksmen, especially among the Patriots, becase the grooved, or "rifled," barrel was more accurate than a musket.

sachet A small bag containing herbs or spices and used for the pleasant aroma or to repel pests.

Stars and Stripes Any American flag with alternating red and white stripes and white stars on a blue field.

tree nails Pegs used in place of metal nails.

tricorn A three-sided, or three-cornered, hat worn by men in the 1700s.

Union Jack The flag of Great Britain.

BIBLIOGRAPHY

Suzanne I. Barchers and Patricia C. Marden. *Cooking Up U.S. History: Recipes and Research to Share with Children.* Chicago: Teachers Ideas Press, 1991.

Marshall Davidson. *Life in America*, 2 vols. Boston: Houghton Mifflin, 1951.

David C. King. *America's Story, Book 2: Forming a New Nation, 1750–1801.* Littleton, Mass.: Sundance, 1996.

Jean Lipman and Alice Winchester. T*he Flowering of American Folk Art, 1776–1876.* Philadelphia: Running Press, 1987.

Eugene F. Provenzo and Asterie Baker Provenzo. *Easy-to-Make Old-Fashioned Toys.* New York: Dover Publications, 1979.

L. Edward Purcell and David W. Burg. *The World Almanac of the American Revolution.* New York: World Almanac, 1992.

Laura Ross. *Hand Puppets: How to Make and Use Them.* New York: Dover Publications, 1989.

George F. Scheer and Hugh F. Rankin. *Rebels and Redcoats: The American Revolution Through the Eyes of Those Who Fought and Lived It.* New York: The World Publishing Company, 1957.

Amelia Simmons. *The First American Cookbook: A Facsimile of "American Cookery," 1796.* New York: Dover Publications, 1958.

Susan Barrows Swan. *Plain and Fancy: American Women and Their Needlework, 1700–1850.* New York: Holt, Rinehart & Winston, 1977.

Richard Wheeler, ed., *Voices of 1776: The Story of the American Revolution in the Words of Those Who Were There.* New York: Penguin Books, 1991.

Ola Elizabeth Winslow, ed. *Harper's Literary Museum: Early American Writings.* New York: Harper & Brothers, 1927.

Meredith Wright. *Everyday Dress of Rural America, 1783–1800.* New York: Dover Publications, 1992.

Carole Yaeger. *Yankee Folk Crafts.* Dublin, N.H : Yankee Publications, 1988.

INDEX